WE FIGHT MONSTERS
HOW TWO JUNKIES BROUGHT HOPE TO THE WORLD'S DARKEST CORNERS BY LAUNCHING A WAR TO END ADDICTION, EXPLOITATION, AND TRAFFICKING

BEN OWEN

JESSICA OWEN

We Fight Monsters Books

USA

© 2025 Ben and Jessica Owen. All Rights Reserved.

DISCLAIMER

All of the stories in this book are true, though names have been changed to protect the guilty.

We dedicate this book to all those still sick and suffering, and to their saviors, the rare ones who raise their hands screaming, "Here am I; Send Me!", and then run headlong into the fires of hell carrying buckets of water for those trapped in the flames.

ABOUT POPPIES AND SPARROWS

FLANDERS FIELDS

I got a tattoo in Buckhead, Atlanta, with multiple poppies once Jess and I applied for our non-profit, Flanders Fields, in 2021. That name came from a poem written by Lieutenant Colonel John McCrea in 1915 after losing a friend in the Battle of Ypres in World War I. After the terrible fighting was over, the soldiers buried their dead where they lay, and McCrea saw poppies growing on the field shortly after. His poem influenced the use of the poppy as a symbol of remembrance by militaries around the world.

We chose our first non-profit's name because of the connection between Veterans and poppies, since heroin is made from the flower. We wanted something to represent the remembrance of veterans, their struggle in the wars of their country as they bled for their nation, and the addiction that often followed. It was interesting that Flanders Fields cut its teeth as a non-profit helping Afghan vets, a country known for opium and poppies.

In January 2022, Jess and I got tattoos on our left arms: a single poppy flower, the symbol we adopted for Flanders Fields. We were representing Black Rifle Co. in Las Vegas for SHOT Show (a major gun convention), when Robert, our business partner, had the idea to get the tattoos. He got the first one followed by two recovering Air Force vets who had come to help out. Since then, many other supporters of our organization, inspired by the commitment, have gotten the poppy tattoo.

IN FLANDERS FIELDS BY LIEUTENANT COLONEL JOHN MCCREA

In Flanders fields, the poppies blow
Between the crosses, row on row,
That mark our place; and in the sky
The larks, still bravely singing, fly
Scarce heard amid the guns below.

We are the Dead. Short days ago
We lived, felt dawn, saw sunset glow,
Loved and were loved, and now we lie,
In Flanders fields.

Take up our quarrel with the foe:
To you from failing hands we throw
The torch; be yours to hold it high.
If ye break faith with us who die
We shall not sleep, though poppies grow
In Flanders fields.

WE FIGHT MONSTERS

Our second non-profit was called "We Fight Monsters" to represent the challenges (monsters) faced by addicts.

Operation Sparrow was its first mission. That mission was to save

ABOUT POPPIES AND SPARROWS

Miss Texas (Lavoria), a former Army Drill Sergeant who had been raped while stationed in Germany in the 1990s and received an Other Than Honorable discharge because she wouldn't stay quiet. Her life then spiraled into addiction, which led to prostitution and later to sex trafficking.

Unfortunately, we weren't able to locate Miss Texas at that time, but in the process, we encountered and befriended a wide swathe of women in her shoes. Because of Miss Texas, we were able to help many women who had found themselves in over their heads and needing the help of folks who were unafraid of confronting the evils that kept them bound.

The name of Operation Sparrow came from Matthew 10:29-31, which reads,

"Are not two sparrows sold for a penny? Yet not one of them will fall to the ground unperceived by Your Father. And even the hairs of your head are all counted. So, do not be afraid; you are of more value than many sparrows."

Many girls are sold by addicted parents and find themselves still stuck in a life they didn't choose decades later. Others start down that slippery slope during their own addiction. Regardless of how they find themselves there, we are here to get them out when they are willing and ready, no matter the risks involved.

Operation Sparrow and the search for Miss Texas motivated us to make the red sparrow our symbol for We Fight Monsters.

PROLOGUE

By December 2018, my wife Jessica and I had given up.

Our lives were as dark and cold as the winter nights we were spending on the streets. Instead of trying to fix it, we just accepted that we were junkies and that was our life.

At first, we'd been able to indulge our addictions and still hold it all together. We'd make a quick buck, buy dope, run out of dope, then rinse and repeat multiple times a day, every day. Our junkie brains didn't process that servicing a $300–$1,000 per day habit meant we couldn't pay our bills. It wasn't long before the wheels fell off and we lost our businesses, our house, our vehicles, and finally, the innocent victims of our ever-growing madness—our kids.

After that, we were stuck in a never-ending cycle of, "Ben's high and going to jail," or "Ben's clean and Jess is back on pills." It was shitty not being there for our kids, especially our youngest, James, who wasn't lucky enough to be taken in by a family member like the others. Instead, he was with us, being "cared for" by a pair of junkies who'd spent five months on the street, living in dope houses, outside, or in vehicles we'd hustled up.

We *wanted* to do better. We *wanted* to be there for our kids. But all we *could* do was dope. With every move we made centered on heroin and crack, there was no end in sight. Drugs had consumed our entire existence, and that's just the way it was and the way it would always be. Until we made a choice.

Damp, overgrown grass stuck to my sweaty face, tickling my nostrils as I slowly regained consciousness.

Fuck. As I pushed up off the ground and took in my surroundings, I immediately recognized where I was—1428 Woodward Street, a place I had come many times to get my dope—though I had zero memory of how I'd gotten there.

Anxious and confused, I scrubbed my hands across my face, and they came away bloody. Coupled with the stale taste of vodka in the back of my throat, I figured the blood was probably from puking all night. A quick glance down at myself revealed that my hands, shirt, and shorts were also smeared with blood.

Shit, am I hurt? I was honestly too fucked up to tell, but I didn't think so.

Does that mean I hurt someone else? And why am I here? Where are Jess and James? Where's my truck, and my phone?

Panicked thoughts piled up, coming faster and faster, in direct contrast to the serene scene of birds chirping, a dog barking, and kids playing next door.

My head pounded in a way it hadn't in a long time, and I still couldn't remember what had happened or how I'd gotten there. I searched my mind, willing a memory to surface.

Jess! I finally remembered. We'd had a fight. Drunk out of my mind, I decided to get clean and "show her," so I took off, leaving her alone with James.

As I stood there processing, the previous seventy-two hours came back to me in snippets: violence, gunfire, running, ducking and dodging, a dog almost mauling me, my mom crying, my dad yelling at me on the other end of a phone, "Ben, just come home. Buddy boy, please. Just come home."

Home. I needed to go home. But how was I supposed to get there?

I needed dope. Then I'd wake up, call Jess, and figure it out.

For some reason, I couldn't move. I was ten feet from the place where "salvation" waited, but I wasn't stepping towards it. I looked down at my bare feet. They were nearly black, with one big toenail missing, and blood coating my legs.

This isn't me anymore...this was never me.

Then, a strange thing happened. I turned away from the place that had previously provided hope, comfort, and peace for as long as I could remember. I walked in the opposite direction of the drugs that ruined my life, found someone with a phone, and called my dad.

For the first time in my entire life, I had no idea what was going to happen next, and I really didn't care. It wasn't apathy. I just knew everything was going to be okay, if I just. Kept. Walking. Away.

I knew I would get home.

My addiction kept calling to me, whispering the words that had brought me back so many times before.

"What about Jess?"

"What's going to happen to James?"

"You just need to hit a good one, and you'll be able to think clearly and hustle like you need to."

"Don't keep walking that way. You know you're going to change your mind, and then you'll just have to figure out how to get back here."

"You just need a drink. You're in DTs and will have another heart attack. If you're going to quit, you can't quit cold turkey, Ben, you know this."

Nope. It was all lies.

This time, I would embrace the truth.

This time, I was going *home*.

A Greyhound bus took me to Atlanta. During a stop somewhere in Tennessee, I threw away a crack pipe and a few syringes, determined to be done. When I arrived, someone tried to sell me crack as soon as I stepped off the bus. Obviously, I looked pretty rough. I had money in my pocket...but as far as I was concerned, that part of my life was over.

My parents picked me up and took me home. At 37 years old, I was completely unable to function. I'd had a beautiful family, a huge house, and successful businesses, but now I was nothing.

And that was just fine. For the first time, I accepted my insignificance in this world, and any semblance of ego I'd held onto was gone.

A week later, I got on another Greyhound back to Memphis and brought Jess and James to Georgia in our $700 truck that had stolen plates. Driving down the highway, behind me was the city that had brought my family so much pain, and I took a photo in the rearview mirror that I eventually posted on Facebook with the tag, *I'm leaving this place in the rearview for good.*

My mind felt clear for the first time in a long while, but I had a feeling what I had written wasn't true.

"Jess, I think God wants me to go back to Memphis. I don't think my 'work' there is done." I glanced over at her.

"Work? What work?" she asked, smiling.

What a ridiculous thing to say. I hadn't worked in more than a year. I laughed out loud, looked at her again, and then we both burst out laughing.

After we calmed down, the rest of the drive was quiet, with Jess and the baby eventually falling asleep. Still, my mind was racing. Even though the idea was absurd, that thought never left. Somehow, I knew I would be back, and I would make a difference.

CHAPTER ONE
NOT SMART ENOUGH

EVERY ADULT I ENCOUNTERED CONSIDERED ME EXTREMELY intelligent; "gifted" is what they called it at school. I had a vocabulary of over a hundred words before my first birthday and was reading on a fifth-grade level in kindergarten. As cool as that sounds, that "gift" made growing up very difficult. I never fit in anywhere. Mentally, I wasn't on the same level as my peers, but emotionally I wasn't on the same level as the adults I carried on conversations with. This left me as a chronic odd-man-out in school.

As a kid, I spent my free time reading the encyclopedias we had in our home. I had a voracious appetite for knowledge and wanted to teach myself everything I could. My grandmother worked as a librarian at a community college in Columbus, GA. She often took me to work when she babysat me, and I spent hours reading every book I could get my hands on. When I was six, I asked my parents where babies came from, and they tried to feed me their bullshit story. But I knew they were lying because I'd already read all about it. Santa Claus, the Easter Bunny, and most other fairy tales told to normal kids didn't work on me.

When I was ten, I got my hands on the autobiography of South African surgeon Christiaan Barnard—the man who performed the world's first successful heart transplant. After reading that book, I saw only one potential path for my future. I announced to my parents I wanted to go to Harvard and become a cardiovascular surgeon. For most kids, this statement would probably have been met with knowing looks exchanged between the parents and perhaps some inconsequential and placating "Oh, that's nice, sweetie." My parents knew better.

"That's fantastic, Ben!" my mom told me. She was an industrial engineer by trade, but she was my best friend and fostered my love of learning, my love of knowledge, and my love of whatever I was obsessed with at any given moment. Even on the infrequent occasions I got in trouble, she came up with creative punishments designed to teach me new things, such as volunteering at the zoo. "Well, we'd better get their address so you can write to them, don't you think?" Only my mother would encourage a ten-year-old boy to write Harvard University in order to pursue his dreams.

Write them I did, and to my astonishment, I got a letter back from the university president himself. For the next couple of years, we were pen pals, and my Doogie Howser-esque dreams seemed to be not only feasible, but probable.

Around the age of twelve, I got my hands on a medical text with color photos depicting what cardiovascular surgeons actually did—open heart surgery. The gore and descriptions made me nauseous, so I changed my future medical aspirations to neurosurgery. I figured the brain had less blood and would be more palatable to work on.

Never one to doubt my potential, my dad, who was a former Army Ranger and now worked for Pfizer, connected me with a world-renowned neurologist at the University of Mississippi Medical Center in Jackson, where I established myself in an unofficial internship. Every day after school, I would go to Dr. Angel Leis's office and observe how the staff worked on lab animals, absorbing all the things going on around me. They were researching a phenomenon known as the subcutaneous silent period.

Essentially, when your body is exposed to painful stimuli, the synapses in your brain actually create an interrupt and stop your muscle signals from going from the axon down the dendrite to your muscle fibers. This reflex developed in Neanderthals so that when they grabbed something like a sharp rock or a hot object, they let go within milliseconds, before the brain can even consciously process that it is in pain. In other words, we'd evolved an ability to avert pain before we even realized we were experiencing it. The silent period in the nerve signal is there so that humans cannot physiologically continue to grasp something that is causing pain.

I started making connections in my life with the medical studies I observed in the lab. My grandmother, the librarian, had been diagnosed with early onset Alzheimer's, and I wondered what the silent period would look like in a person with that sort of neurological disorder. I pitched the idea to my mom, and she helped me craft a study. Then I sat down with my dad, and we talked through it until I had a coherent concept.

A few weeks later, I presented my idea to Dr. Leis.

"So, you're hypothesizing that certain disorders would create an abnormality in the silent period," he responded after I explained everything. "Well, let's see if you're right."

I made a formal hypothesis to start the study. Then, with the help of the staff, we asked for volunteers ranging from healthy people to those with various levels of neurological disorders. My mom even volunteered. We began with a controlled experiment that included five test subjects and later expanded to a broader sample before spinning off into a very large clinical study.

To gather information on how the silent period presented in each case, we hooked patients up to leads and shocked them. As a twelve-year-old, I administered the shocks, analyzed brain waves on an electroencephalograph to see the patients' autonomic response to painful stimuli, and recorded all the data.

In the end, we discovered patients with neurological disorders like Parkinson's and Alzheimer's presented with a delay in, or absence of, that silent period. This discovery was particularly useful because it allowed doctors to assess the efficacy of treatments in patients suffering from those conditions. I wrote an article on the experiment, which Dr. Leis helped me submit to a medical publication. Later that year, I presented it at the Mississippi State Science Fair, where I took first place. I remember everybody at the fair saying, "This kid is going to cure cancer someday."

They were wrong, though.

In fact, by the time my article came out in the journal, *Neurology,* a year later, I was locked up in a rehabilitation center.

Being smart might have been my biggest downfall. Maybe I was too smart for my own good. Too smart to listen to anyone else because I thought I knew better.

For the next twenty-five years, I made mistake after mistake, slowly circling the drain of my life, and almost losing everything.

Ben with mom, Melanie Owen

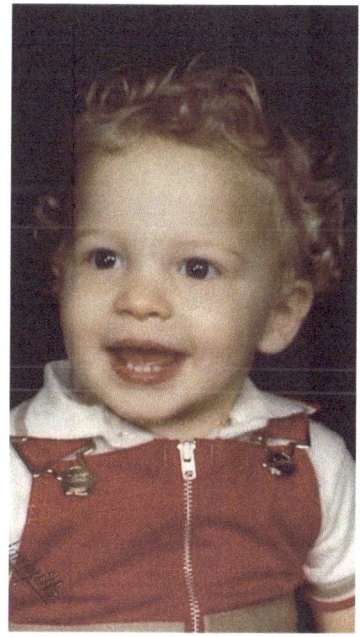

Ben Owen

Ben, brother Cody, and dad Steve

Ben with dad, Steve Owen

WE FIGHT MONSTERS

Ben, age 14, right before being locked up in treatment for the first time.

CHAPTER TWO

BIG MISTAKE

JULY 2014

On July 4, 2014, I watched my wife, Erin, drive away with my five children. I considered going after her for a minute but was too dope-sick to do much of anything before I got my fix. Once I was done puking, I made my way out to the garage and fired up my '68 GTO. My plan was to head to South Memphis, get un-sick, and then figure out how to get my wife and kids back.

Erin had been my first girlfriend. I met her on a church hayride when I was twelve and she was thirteen. Throughout the years, she'd remained someone who loved me despite my faults, who had been there through my alcoholism and drug addiction, seen me through rehab, and stuck with me through all the stupid shit I'd done for the ten years of our marriage. And now, finally, she'd had enough. I'm honestly surprised she made it as long as she did. The last ten months had been an ever-escalating series of disasters. My business was in shambles, my health was failing, and my finances were completely depleted. I was a shell of the man she married, and even that was a generous label.

I pulled out of the driveway, destined for Shady Lane, a journey I had repeated three times a day, every day for the last nine months. My dependence had progressed to the point that if I didn't have heroin every eight hours, I got dope-sick. But literally every single time I went to the trap house, I'd tell myself it was the last time and only bought what I needed for that high. I believed myself every single time. So great was my delusion of still having a semblance of control over my life. I truly wanted to be a father to my kids, a husband to my wife, and a leader to my employees.

"I'll make the hard changes. Tomorrow." I would tell myself over and over, meaning it with all my heart. But tomorrow never came.

The light at Central and East Parkway turned red as I was about twenty yards from it, but I was far too sick to slow down, not this close to salvation. Instead, I dropped into second and punched it, feeling a brief moment of joy remembering I still had a badass hot rod. Brief indeed. I didn't see the truck until it was caving in the side of my precious GTO, which spun out of control and skidded into a light pole in the median.

The smell of gasoline and an acrid smoke surrounded me as I regained consciousness, and the heat of a fire added urgency to my desire to escape the wreckage. My face had hit the steering wheel so hard that my front teeth went through my lip. Now, the steering wheel was bent downward, pinning my legs. I saw bones sticking out of my right foot.

I couldn't move, and I remember thinking, almost in slow motion, "This can't be it, I'm not done".

Removing the fire extinguisher mounted between the seats, I aimed into the back seat where the lamp pole had pushed the ruptured gas tank into the car, and I squeezed the handle. Nothing. Empty. It was getting hot now. I smashed the metal tube through the driver's side window.

BOOM.

Introducing more oxygen into the car had been a terrible idea, but it alerted bystanders that I was still alive. A panhandler that I'd given money to on numerous occasions ran to the car and pulled me out.

I patted my clothes, but somehow, I didn't have a single burn on my body despite a wallet full of melted debit cards and a cooked cell phone. *Shit, all my cash was in the passenger seat.* I limped back towards the flaming car on my broken foot.

Ammo began to cook off. I could hear sirens coming, and I realized not only was I still dope-sick, but I was only a mile from where I needed to be. Compound fracture be damned, I started trying to get away from the scene while I could.

An ambulance skidded to a halt beside me.

"Hey, man, you ok?", yelled an EMT, jumping out.

"I'm good," I told him, limping toward my destination.

"You are definitely not good, buddy."

I wasn't stopping. I was a man on a mission. I soon learned that Memphis Fire employs men who take their work as seriously as I took my mission, and found myself being forced to the ground, strapped to a backboard, and loaded into the ambulance.

"Erin...the GTO's gone and I'm hurt."

She hung up on me. I don't know that I expected any different. After cutting off all my charred clothes, they discharged me wearing nothing but paper scrubs and an orthotic boot on my foot. I called a cab, picked up some beer with the smoldering cash I'd been able to recover from the passenger seat, and I limped to the dope house.

Over the next week, Erin cut off my money supply by reporting all of our debit and credit cards as stolen, and I accepted that I was a legitimate junkie by acting the part. Pawning my valuables was the only "logical" thing to do at this point, and I had quite a valuable collection of firearms. I rationalized the hit in value by telling myself I'd buy them all back with the $35,000 insurance check from my GTO when it came. The next few weeks became a cycle of pawning guns, buying dope, and buying the guns back as money became available. Though my cards were cut off, I could still withdraw cash from the bank in person, and on July 28, 2014, I took out $12,000, got my dope, and bought back eight firearms from the pawnshop.

I had a makeshift shooting range behind my warehouse where I'd blow off steam, and that day felt like a good day to do just that. I was still trying to quit the heroin, so I delayed using my recent purchase, stretching the time and allowing myself to get as sick as I could tolerate before touching it. After a few hours of shooting, I drove back to my house with all my dope, two legally purchased suppressors, a submachine gun, a pistol, an AK rifle, and a huge amount of ammo.

When the sirens went off behind me, a cold chill went down my spine. Memphis Police. *This won't end well,* went through my head as I tried to determine how to hide an arsenal and a pile of dope.

"License and registra...," the cop began.

"Holy shit! Get out of the car, now!" His gun was out and pointed straight at me.

Within seconds, I was cuffed. He pulled the dope out of my pockets then stuffed me in the back of his car. It was immediately apparent that these officers had no understanding of the laws around suppressors or machine guns, and instead of reading the ATF paperwork I had on me showing that I legally and legitimately owned the guns, they started asking me which military installation I'd stolen them from.

I was in for a very long day. Being only a mile from my home, and convinced I was not only a drug dealer, but an arms dealer as well, the ever-growing crowd of law enforcement convinced me that things would go much easier on me if I granted them permission to shift the scene from the traffic stop to my residence. I obliged as the only illegal thing I had was the heroin and crack in my pocket, and I was getting too dope-sick to think very clearly.

Within minutes of being transported home, it felt like half of West Tennessee's law enforcement capacity was being diverted to my house. Tennessee Bureau of Investigations, ATF, DEA, West TN Violent Crime and Drug Task Force, MPD's Organized Crime Unit, and at least thirty vehicles from said agencies convened on my house.

I was in deep shit.

BEN OWEN & JESSICA OWEN

Ben and Erin

Ben, Erin, Joseph, Jacob, Jackson, Lily, and Joshua

Ben's 1968 GTO

Ben's totalled 1968 GTO

CHAPTER THREE
BACK TO HELL

AUGUST 2014

"Okay, Ben. Who's your plug and who are you selling to?" The detectives acted as though they had Pablo Escobar on their hands. I get it - house on a golf course, easily a hundred-thousand-dollar firearm collection, multiple vehicles - but I was legitimately just a junkie.

"What the fuck are you talking about? I've never sold dope a day in my life. This is *mine*. For the love of God, hand me that H and a rig and I'll prove it."

They laughed at that. I had six grams of heroin, enough to kill an elephant, and an additional three grams of crack cocaine, which could revive said elephant. They certainly had enough to charge me with intent to sell, except it just wasn't true.

An hour later, they weren't laughing anymore as withdrawals *really* set in. I think that's when they first began to believe my story, and the tone of the interrogation shifted not so subtly. I already knew where this was heading. I'd heard plenty about the "snitch station" on Shelby Drive, and sure enough, that's where we ended up. They left me handcuffed in a frigid cell on a cement bench for what felt like hours, really letting that dope sickness set in.

Smart, I thought to myself. There was no way I'd ever follow through with what they wanted, but if agreeing to become a confidential informant got this case dropped and me a free man, I'd agree to do just about anything at this point.

After what seemed like an eternity, the detective finally walked in holding the CI offer as expected.

"Where do I sign?" I asked without hesitation.

They gave me their spiel and set expectations. I'd have to "give up" my dealers, do controlled buys, blah blah blah - wasn't gonna happen, but at that point I wasn't worried about getting out of anything but that cell. We made our deal, and they took the handcuffs off and gave me my truck back, minus the guns. As I slid behind the wheel, I noticed they'd left my crack on the passenger seat—not sure if that was intentional. Unfortunately, I was dope sick, and the only thing that could cure that was heroin. So, I had to run back to South Memphis before I could finally go home.

"Do you know why I pulled you over?", said the Shelby County deputy sheriff. Then, he saw my passenger seat and drew his weapon. "Out of the truck, now!" Déjà vu.

After the Memphis PD let me go, I drove straight back to the Melrose trap house, purchased the same amount of drugs, and headed home. Turns out, it was a terrible decision for many reasons beyond the obvious ones, because I ran a red light and was pulled over across the street from where I had been arrested earlier that day.

To add insult to injury, I was still dope-sick. I wanted to get home safely before using, so I'd toughed it out. The Shelby County guys did not mess around. They were rough and didn't give a fuck when I told them I was a confidential informant. I went straight to jail.

Weirdly enough, Shelby County didn't have my earlier arrest by Memphis PD in their system, so I was only booked on these new dope charges (no gun charges yet) and only had a $10,000 bond. It didn't matter, though, because I knew no one would pay to get me out. Dope-sick and delusional, I decided to minimize my problems by lying and telling them I didn't drink, all in the hopes of getting myself a pretrial diversion instead of jail time. This was just another mistake in a long line of mistakes. Instead of sending me to the jail's detox pod, they stuck me in what's referred to as "Lower Level", which is literally underneath the jail - no joke - without anything to deal with the withdrawals which were causing me to hallucinate and have seizures. Coming off alcohol, heroin, and cocaine all at the same time with no medical intervention was no fun, not to mention, life threatening.

    I don't remember much of the first week because I was so dope-sick. When they threw me into jail, I looked like I had just come out of a concentration camp. My usual weight was about 175 pounds, but at that time I weighed 138. When I finally realized where I was, I found myself in a big room with thirty-two bunk beds, and as one of the only white guys in a pod of over sixty men. This didn't look like it was going to end well.

I was beyond desperate for answers, any lifeline, a glimmer of hope. I'd seen the affidavit when they booked me, and knew I had a second case (which was actually the first case, from the first stop that day) that was getting dropped on me any day with fourteen felony charges. I was looking at a decade if convicted.

    My calls with Erin were understandably full of vitriol and resentment, my parents were completely lost as to how to navigate this process, and I began to realize I had isolated myself to the point of finally being alone to suffer the consequences of my decisions. My court dates only furthered my fear and confusion. Veterans Court didn't want to give me a chance because they could see the pending gun charges, and it was the same with all the other potential pre-trial options.

    "The Feds are going to pick this up," became a constant reply from anyone looking at my case. For those fortunate souls unfamiliar with the judicial process, that means you're fucked. Feds don't take cases they can't get a conviction on.

    "21 Bunk, Owen!" When I heard my name called a few days later, I walked to the pod officer's desk, who motioned towards the Sally Port, where two more COs were waiting.

"What's going on?" I asked.

"Man, what you got going on?", he barked back. "You caught another case. AOC, baby. Add On Charges waiting on you downstairs. They got two class A felonies, a few B's, a half dozen D's. How much dope they get you with, lil bro?"

I knew this moment was coming, but class-A felonies for my own drugs? None of this made any sense. But there was absolutely nothing I could do about it. I knew my bond was about to go to six figures. Not that it mattered. They could have raised it to a million dollars, and it would have been the same outcome. I was fingerprinted again, listened to the charges they read to me, signed the affidavit, and was taken back to my pod, where I hit my bunk, and prayed that God would let me die in my sleep.

"21 Bunk, Owen!" the pod officer yelled the next morning. I was becoming popular.

Fuck. What now? I thought.

"Pack your shit!"

Oh fuck!

This was it, the Feds had come. I just knew it.

God fucking damn it! I'm done. It's over.

They took me down to Release, which is also where you go to be turned over to other agencies, and I asked the lady, "What agency is picking me up?"

"What?", she replied, looking at me like I had six eyes. "You're being released."

"Right, but to whose custody? Who's picking me up?" I was convinced it was the Department of Justice, FBI, or ATF; take your pick from the alphabet.

"I don't give a fuck who picks you up. Walk. You got legs. You through here. You made bond."

I was convinced she was fucking with me, a seemingly common pastime of the pod officers at 201 Poplar. Nobody was going to post my bond. I'd accepted that. I'd burned literally every bridge.

My skepticism remained strong until they cut my wristband off, sent me through the sally port, and there was nobody on the other side waiting for me. I was free.

I called Erin. "Thank you so fucking much. I'm so sorry. We're gonna work this out. We're gon—"

"Ben, how the *fuck* do you have your phone?", she screamed over me. "Are you out of fucking jail?"

"Didn't you bond me out?", I asked, completely baffled by her response.

"Fuck no. And by the way, I want a divorce." Then she hung up. As much crap as I'd put her through, it didn't come as a surprise, nor could I blame her, but I sure as hell didn't want that.

About that time, my dope boy started calling me. He had posted the $450 for my $10,000 bond. It made sense; while I was in jail, he was losing $800 a day from his number one customer. Unfortunately for him, after my time in jail, I'd detoxed from heroin and had no desire to start it back. I'd lived through that hell once, and that was enough. I needed to beat this case, fix my marriage, and be there for my kids.

Evidently, my six-figure bond hadn't made it through the system yet. I was one lucky motherfucker, that's for sure.

I still had a broken foot, and post-acute withdrawals wracked my body, but I was out of jail. My home was twenty miles away in the suburbs, but the dope house on Shady Lane was only two miles away. With no one else to call and my truck impounded, I limped to the dope house. I spent that night in the house on Shady, managed to stay clear of heroin, but gave back in to crack within minutes of arriving on my old block. In my twisted way of thinking, that was a win. In reality, I spiraled more on crack than I ever had on heroin.

"You're a piece of shit," I told my reflection.

I had spent a lot of time at Shady Lane before Erin left, buying dope, watching the insanity around there, and just hanging out. It had no running water, no power, and a huge roach problem. There was a mirror in the living room above the fireplace, and every day before I left, I would look into that mirror and tell myself, "You're a piece of shit."

When you make bond, you'll almost always be assigned a hearing the very next day so the Judge can give you the conditions of your bond, eyeball you, get a feel for your risk level, etc. So, the next day, I woke up ready to go for my hearing, dry shaved in that mirror with a rusty razor someone had left behind, and just like always, I looked myself in the eye. "You're a piece of shit."

Miss Texas came up behind me, high as a kite. "Honey," she told me in a sluggish southern twang. "You know, talking to yourself that way ain't gonna end in anything good." Then she gave me a hug and sent me out the door. My running buddy, Smokey, a 1/9 Marine and Vietnam Veteran, gave me a ride to court and dropped me off with zero time to spare.

I still had the crack pipe that I'd used the night before in my pocket, and I threw it into the bushes as I entered the building, where I greeted the bailiff with a smile that was met with a look I didn't like at all.

"What's your name?", she asked.

I told her.

"Judge, we got Owen!", she yelled. "Mr. Owen, have a seat in that chair with the red handcuffs on the armrest," the bailiff told me, then tightened the cuffs around my wrist before she even finished her sentence.

The judge told me there was a mix-up in jail, that I had add-on charges from the night before I bonded out, and the bond that was paid was only for the smaller case. The other case included "some very serious charges."

"Well, fuck," I said. "I literally just checked into a halfway house last night."

The trap house on Shady Lane just happened to be owned by a guy named Rodney who'd schemed the state into thinking he was running a registered, legit, non-profit halfway house, when really, he was bleeding social services while providing dope to his tenants. In hindsight, it was actually a pretty brilliant move; he got the state to keep a roof over his customers' heads and pay him to do it.

In a shocking moment of seemingly good fortune, the prosecutor didn't have any objection to letting me go back to my "halfway house". The judge agreed because the warrant hadn't been issued yet, and she didn't really have reason to hold me if the prosecution didn't object.

"Listen up, Mr. Owen," she told me in open court. "The warrant will probably go out today and will include nine felonies, including multiple drug trafficking charges and six counts of possession of a firearm during the commission of a dangerous felony. So, just be ready when the officers come to serve this warrant. They're not gonna treat you very kindly."

"They never do," I replied.

She smiled. "I bet they don't."

Then they let me go.

God gave me a chance to do what's right that day. I could have caught a ride home, cleaned up, got my life back together, and reunited with my wife and kids.

Instead, I walked back to Shady Lane.

"What the fuck are you doing here?", Erin shouted at me.

"I need my truck," was all I said. I was still getting over my surprise at finding her home.

When she'd left, she had taken the kids to her dad's place. Since I'd been gone so long, she'd moved back in, probably thinking I was dead, still in jail, or stoned out of my mind somewhere. Rodney, the owner of the Shady Lane house, had offered me a job demolishing and refurbishing the newest additions to his slumlord portfolio in order to pay for my crack that he supplied. For five days straight I didn't sleep, just worked and smoked crack, then decided I needed some wheels and took the bus most of the way home. We lived way out in the suburbs and the bus line stopped a few miles short, so back to walking on the broken foot I went.

Erin was not happy. "Shelby County was just here, trying to serve a warrant. They scared the hell out of the kids, all because their daddy can't get his shit together. Get out. Get. The. Fuck. OUT!"

Her anger hurt, but I couldn't blame her. "I'm just here to pick up my truck," I told her again. "Then I'll leave."

"Fuck no," she spat. "You think I'm going to let you have one of our vehicles so you can go sell it for dope? Get. Out."

Shamefaced, I turned and left without a word. She was right about everything. Not the part about selling the truck for drugs, but I did want to make it easier to buy them. But what she was really right about was the poor decisions I was making and the horrible daddy I was being. I was hurting my family and killing myself, and I knew it.

It only took a few days for my shame to be replaced by selfishness.

Who was Erin to tell me whether I could drive one of the vehicles I'd purchased? She didn't pay for shit. She was a stay-at-home mom while I earned all the money. If I wanted to drive my fucking truck, I would.

At two in the morning, I showed up at my house and "stole" my truck back.

Within three days, I had wrecked it six times. It was running on the spare tire, the front bumper was hanging off, and both side view mirrors were gone.

I wanted to change; I really did. Everywhere I went, everything I did, destruction followed. Every day, I promised to do better, but I just couldn't stop.

News clip from arrest 7/28/2014

CHAPTER FOUR
SECOND CHANCES

SEPTEMBER 2014

"You need to go, my brother," said Smokey, who was in charge of the rooming house on Shady Lane. I had real big boy warrants out for my arrest, and if Rodney found out, it wouldn't be pretty. Bringing that kind of heat to his block wouldn't go unpunished. Miss Texas tried to cover for me, but my case ended up on the news. Everyone knew the danger I was bringing by staying there. It wouldn't just be me going to jail when the U.S. Marshals busted down the door. After all, it was supposed to be a halfway house with no drugs allowed which it obviously wasn't.

I honestly had nowhere else to go, but I knew Smokey was right.

"You leave him alone," said Miss Texas. And that was the end of that discussion. Smokey may have been "in charge", but for whatever reason, he deferred to Miss Texas.

My life was looking shittier every day. Erin hadn't let me see my kids in weeks, but I knew I had no business being around them. I was in no shape to be the father they needed.

I looked into the mirror again, but this time I held a K-Bar knife.

"You're a piece of shit," I told my reflection as tears fell. "You don't deserve them."

I put the knife to my throat and prepared to free my family of the burden I'd become, when a warm hand covered mine.

"Honey, give that to me."

I let her take it, then collapsed to the floor, crying and gasping for breath.

Miss Texas sat down beside me and put the knife on the floor, then put my head in her lap. "You're gonna be okay. This too shall pass," she told me. She scratched my head and held me until I calmed down. Then we smoked crack together.

"Owen, I explained this to you last time you were in custody. There's no way in hell I can take your case," said the Veterans' Court director. "The feds are coming for you because of the gun charges."

I'd been arrested a few weeks after I tried to kill myself. Erin had finally agreed to let me see the kids, and the West TN Drug Task Force pulled me and one of Rodney's guys over when I was on my way for the visit. They cut me a break, though, and didn't charge me for any drugs they found at the time. They just took me in on that outstanding warrant.

My case was reset for a week later in drug court, where the judge initially kicked me out of his courtroom and sent me back to my cell. A week later, I was brought before him again. He looked me straight in the eyes and asked, "Owens, do you want to stay clean?" Normally, I'd correct "Owens" to "Owen" but this wasn't the time for that. I knew this judge had the power to set me free and to get me some help… the two things I wanted more than anything in the world.

"Yes, sir. I do." I wanted to be clean and get my family back. I wanted my life back. I truly did.

My parents had driven over from North Georgia for the hearing and were in the courtroom. Judge Dwyer called them both up, looked them dead in their eyes, and asked them if they would make certain I showed up to court the next day. Of course, they affirmed that they would, and he released me on my own recognizance into their custody - in other words, the Judge waived my bond and let me out. As I turned to go back to my cell and await my release call, the Judge whispered sternly, "Owens…if you fuck me, I'll fuck you back. Don't forget that."

A few hours later, the pod officer yelled, "Owen, pack your shit!" I knew I was about to be free. My parents were outside waiting. We all went to a hotel to get a good night's sleep before the big court hearing the next day which would decide my fate. In that moment, I was legitimately committed to staying sober, turning my life around, and becoming the daddy and husband I once was.

Still, the second they were asleep, I walked over to Joe's Crab Shack and got a few beers with the seventeen dollars I had, then came back without anyone ever knowing. Miraculously, the screening for alcohol and drugs the next day came back negative, and we proceeded to drug court for my assessment hearing. I knew I needed to be accepted; drug court offered judicial diversion and a chance to have my charges expunged if I stayed sober and completed a rigorous eighteen-month program. I'd been to rehab before and knew the right things to say to convince them I was a good candidate for this opportunity.

While that may sound like manipulation, and it was, it was also genuine on my part. I needed this help. And I wanted a clean criminal record. After a few hours of going back and forth with attorneys, counselors, social workers, and the Judge, I was accepted into the Shelby County Drug Court program, and my first requirement was to complete an undetermined length of stay at Cocaine and Alcohol Abuse Prevention (CAAP), a rehab facility in East Memphis. I badly wanted to see my wife and kids before I went in, and Erin was open to that. She even agreed to take me to CAAP and stay with me through the intake process. She was very supportive and friendly, but also still very firm that we were getting divorced.

I spent 54 days at CAAP and was finally released in November 2014. Erin insisted that I couldn't come home, so I went to a halfway house called Rebos—sober, spelled backwards—but I had no fucking desire to be there. Homesickness assaulted me in a way I'd never felt before. I missed my kids, I didn't want a divorce, and I didn't want to lose the business I'd almost killed myself trying to build.

I started a business called Retech a few years prior, selling parts from broken TV sets to supply the repair industry. It had been pretty successful until I started getting high. Somehow, despite all my time in jail and rehab, my business had not collapsed. The rent on the warehouse had not been paid, and no customers had been taken care of, but it was salvageable. Still, it was a fucking struggle every second of every day to do what I was supposed to do—stay sober and go to work.

Drug court required daily attendance at 12-step meetings plus an intensive outpatient program. They also administered random drug screens with only an hour's notice. Without a vehicle, making it to all the appointments was damn near impossible.

Fortunately, my new AA sponsor was a car salesman, My parents lent me $5,000 to buy an old, '63 Impala, which was a flaming piece of shit. But it looked cool and ran.

The owner of Rebos, Tony, saw me drive up in my new car. "You're a dumbass," he told me. He was furious.

I shook my head. "What? I love old cars. This thing is awesome! It's going to make my life a whole lot easier."

"That's the last thing you need right now, Mr. Big Shot." As a recovered alcoholic himself, he had a very different way of looking at recovery. He believed I needed to embrace the suck. "You need to experience the harshness of life and be humbled, not ride down easy street. That's the only way this works. You need to learn to depend on the people who are here to see you through your recovery."

In retrospect, he wasn't wrong, but I wasn't interested in any of that. All I wanted to do was prove to Tony, Erin, my parents, and everyone else that I could do things my way and still succeed.

Ben's 1963 Impala

CHAPTER FIVE

DIVORCE

NOVEMBER 2014

"I HATE THIS PART OF MY JOB," THE BAILIFF TOLD ME AS HE held out a sheet of paper. The relief I initially felt upon realizing I wasn't being arrested evaporated as devastation swept in. Erin had served me with a restraining order.

What the fuck? I'd never laid a hand on Erin or my kids, never even threatened to.

What had started as a standard, scheduled court appearance had turned into a nightmare. The initial panic and fear I'd felt when I thought the bailiff was approaching to arrest me returned in force. My life was fucked. I'd been trying—to stay sober, to stay working, to meet the requirements of drug court and my sober home—all so I could get a piece of paper telling me I couldn't see or speak to my wife or children.

Lost in my feelings, I headed over to the trap house on Melrose Street, where I got drunk and high on heroin. Despite having caved to my feelings and addictions, I still wasn't ready to completely set fire to my life, so I made sure to leave in time to get back to the sober home before my 10:00 pm curfew. Unfortunately, my shit box car wouldn't start.

Fuck it, I thought.

I stayed up all night smoking crack and doing heroin. The next morning, by some miracle, the Impala cranked, and I pulled into the halfway house at 6 am. When Tony questioned me, I claimed that I'd had a job interview, but that went over like a turd in the punchbowl. He hauled me straight to court where the judge threw my ass back in jail.

Two weeks later, I called Erin from jail so that I could talk to my kids and wish them a happy Thanksgiving. Technically, I probably shouldn't have, considering the restraining order, but it was bad enough spending the holiday in jail without the added pain of not being able to speak to my family.

"I'm sorry about the restraining order." Guilt threaded Erin's voice as it came through the phone. "My lawyer insisted on it, and as much as I hate hurting you, I have to protect the kids. They need consistency in their lives, and this cycle of you being in and out of jail, sober one minute and high the next, it's just not healthy for any of us." Nothing she said was untrue or unfair, but it still hurt, as did her continued insistence that she wanted the divorce.

Over the next few weeks, I continued to speak to the kids, and each time, Erin and I seemed to be getting along. It gave me renewed hope that maybe I could save our marriage. I'd fucked up—I knew that. But I still loved my wife, and the idea of losing her devastated me.

Just before they released me from jail on December 17, a drug court counselor named Bryan confronted me.

"Aren't you sick of living this way?", he asked me. "Do you want to fucking die, or do you wanna start living again?" He then read me the riot act on what my irresponsible actions were doing to my family, and for some reason, I listened to him. "Look man," he continued, "if you want to live, you need to come back to this courtroom tomorrow; let's figure it out." Something about the way he spoke lodged in my brain, but I had other things to worry about as I stepped out of the jail.

The judge wouldn't let me go home due to the restraining order, and the halfway house owner wouldn't let me back there because I had broken every rule he gave me in less than a week. With no place to go, I finally called my dad.

"What the fuck do I do? My choices are to sleep in my car in

December and probably die, or go back to the dope track where I know I have a place to sleep, but I can't stay clean if I'm out there."

"Ben, go get an extended stay hotel. I'll pay. Just do it." Gratitude overwhelmed me. I'd abused the generosity and patience of my parents for most of my life. Obviously, I'd been hoping my dad would help when I called him, but there'd been no guarantees. I knew my parents were as sick of my shit as Erin was, and there was just as much chance that my dad would tell me to get fucked as there was that he would offer me help.

The next day, Bryan was waiting at the courthouse. He took me to my very first Narcotics Anonymous meeting.

The day after that, I returned to court yet again to address the restraining order.

The judge called Erin up and asked, "When was Ben verbally or physically abusive to you or the children?"

"He was never any of those things," she replied.

The judge stared at her in surprise. "Do you realize you committed perjury by filing this?"

"But I didn't file it," she said, "My attorney did."

The judge immediately threw the restraining order out.

Afterward, I went back to the hotel, and Erin called me. "Ben, your daughter wants to see you."

That tugged at my heartstrings, because I really missed the kids. "Cool," I said. "I'll come right over."

"Well, how about she stays with you at the hotel tonight?"

Over the next week, the five kids took turns staying with me. We had a great time, and it motivated me to get my life back together. Even though it was hard as hell, I complied with all the requirements of the drug court.

Erin invited me over for Christmas, and I thought it might be my chance to show her I'd changed. She'd known me for twenty years, back when I was a punk middle schooler smoking cigarettes, when I was a fifteen-year-old who got sent to Island View rehab for nine months, and through the various trials of our marriage. Through it all, she had been able to forgive me for anything.

After a long conversation that night, she told me that she did want a life together, but there were things we had to work out. Boundaries we needed to set.

Then, on New Year's Eve, I received a call from an attorney who represented the owner of the warehouse where ReTech had been operating, asking why I hadn't gotten my inventory out. Believing the business was an impediment to my sobriety, Erin had lied to me. She'd told me the owner had foreclosed and my inventory had been trashed, when in reality she'd received a letter giving us until midnight on December 31st to get everything out. I completely lost it. There was over a million dollars in inventory and over $30,000 in tools out there. It was 5 pm, and it weighed nearly 30 tons. There was no way I could get everything out in time.

Furious, I threw my phone into the wall and sat down on the floor, unable to speak or move. Years of sacrifice and hard work went down the drain when it didn't have to, and all because she hadn't bothered to tell me about that stupid fucking letter. Suddenly, all the resentment I'd previously let go of—the restraining order, and her general refusal to provide me with the emotional support I needed while I was spiraling in my addiction—all came to the fore. The scales tipped, and suddenly it was me who wasn't so sure I wanted to stay married.

"Ben, please. Running Retech stressed you out so much. The hours you worked were insane. I don't care about you making tons of money. I just want you to be sober, healthy, and here with me and the kids."

"Yeah?", I sneered. "Well, how the fuck are we going to pay for the roof over our heads now?"

Her pleading expression shifted at the vitriol in my tone. "You know what, Ben? If you need to put all this on me, then fine, you go right ahead. But you and I both know the truth. Your business isn't going under just because I waited a week to give you a letter. You're the one who put it in that situation. Did you think everything would just be fine while you spent all your time on the dope track getting high? What did you think was going to happen to the business while you were in jail? Or did you even care? Fuck, I'm tired of your shit. Nothing's ever your fault, Ben. You're always the victim, and I'm your favorite villain."

Her words only pissed me off more. She *was* the villain. Even if I'd messed up, I could have saved Retech. Our livelihood was salvageable from my madness, yet now permanently fucked because of her.

We were both unhappy in our marriage, but we loved each other. In reality, we were very different people. Even if I could stay away from drugs and alcohol this time, my obsessive personality would find something else to latch onto, which would in turn make her unhappy; it was just the way I was built. For my part, I didn't want to be alone, which wasn't fair to Erin, but was the absolute truth. And I knew I had baggage: a history with drugs and five children, which I accepted full responsibility for. I just couldn't see anyone choosing me, given all the negatives. So, I felt stuck in my life. If I didn't want to be alone, I had to be with Erin. Still, being with her stressed me out. We'd known each other since we were kids, but I knew more than anyone all the times I had let her and the kids down.

Additionally, she couldn't understand what I was going through with my addictions, having never been addicted herself. That wasn't the problem, but she just wasn't supportive in the way I needed her to be. One night, she went out with some girlfriends and she came back reeking of alcohol and kissed me. I couldn't believe it. I knew only too well that my home life would lead me back to addiction.

As a result of my inner war, I began avoiding Erin—avoiding being at home at all.

The Melrose trap house "The Door to Hell"

CHAPTER SIX
JESSICA

JANUARY 2015

Life happens to you when you least expect it to.

In January 2015, as I wrestled with my relationship with Erin and we grew further apart, I met someone who would change the direction of my life. She sat across the table from me at a restaurant Bryan had chosen to celebrate his girlfriend's sober anniversary. She was focused on her phone and doing a great job of not interacting with the rest of the people. I'd been attending NA with Bryan regularly ever since he confronted me in court, and I was sober because of it. Despite having been absorbed into his friend group, I'd never met this woman before.

Occasionally she would let out a chuckle as she scrolled through her phone, drawing my attention away from the people around us, but she never looked up or engaged.

"Look at this." Suddenly, she was holding her phone out to me, displaying a tray of cupcakes made to look like vaginas.

"Holy shit," I said. "What the hell?"

"I have no idea how I found this, but it's hilarious."

I burst out laughing. "That's amazing. Can you text that to me?"

She agreed, and I gave her my cell number. This was the first girl who had shown an iota of interest in me in a long time, and it made me smile.

Her name was Jessica, Jess to her friends. I saw her again at the weekly NA meetings, and on Trivia Crack, a game that nearly the whole NA group was a part of.

You must be cheating. No one can win every time.

I smirked when I saw the DM she'd sent me through the game and replied, *And yet...*

One day, a few weeks after we'd first met, I was standing outside the NA meeting next to my '63 Impala when suddenly she was in front of me.

"Who's fucking car is this?", she demanded.

I didn't even see her come up. "Mine," I replied. It turned out she was a classic car fanatic. Who knew? We had a long conversation about cars, rehab, and a ton of other topics. By the time her friend got her attention to leave, Jess was consuming my thoughts.

"A few of us are going to dinner. You want to come with us?", asked Jess.

After that conversation about cars, I realized she was a pretty cool person, but I was trying to focus on my business and sobriety, and I needed to keep my life simple. Also, NA frowned upon dating between the members, though it happened often enough.

"Nah, I'm heading home," I told her.

"Don't be a pussy," said Jess. "You're already halfway there, you're wearing flip-flops. Go change your tampon and come out to eat with us."

"Damn it, okay, fine."

We went to dinner, and she invited me and her friend, Ross, to a Quentin Tarantino movie fest at the local drive-in the next night. Ross didn't show, but I brought a friend named Thomas. With three of us there, it didn't start out like a date, but Thomas got belligerently drunk; he was having some problems at home. So, Jess and I took him home, then came back to the cinema, just her and I talking all night and watching movies.

That was the night that my marriage finally ended for me.

Addicts hate change. Erin and I might not have been happy, but my life was predictable, which I liked. Before that night, I didn't think anyone could overlook all the baggage in my life. And on top of that, none of the women I knew were the type I would want to be with; they were drug addicts, homeless, or criminals.

All that changed as I watched movies and hung out with Jess. New possibilities for my life seemed to materialize. I saw hope.

Wanna go fishing? Jess texted me.

Hell yes! I replied.

Meet me at Shelby Forest this afternoon.

I'm there!

As it turned out, after all the years I had lived in Memphis, I had no idea that place existed. I was dumbfounded. Not only did this girl have a sense of humor, but she had tapped into my greatest love of all time, nature.

I guess you could call that our first date, except that she invited her friend, Ross, and brought her daughter, Madison. Despite Jess's best efforts to get Ross out there, he never showed, and it ended up being just us three. Madison hopped out of the car and immediately a smile hit her face. She shyly said hi as she took in the beauty all around her. Apparently, she loved nature too.

"Forget your poles?" I asked when they got out of the car.

Turns out that she had no idea how to fish.

"I thought we'd just walk around a bit," she replied. I started to put two and two together and assumed that this was a test to see how I got along with her daughter. Challenge accepted.

"Sounds great to me," I told her with a smile.

On the surface, it might not seem like this was the best date. We were immediately and constantly swarmed by mosquitos and had to turn back after about an hour. Madison was clueless as to her part in the plan, she just enjoyed being outside. But I engaged with her throughout, talking about the wilderness. I'd been a Boy Scout and grown up in the woods, after all.

We ended up pivoting plans to some wooded swampy areas, hoping to find some snakes or turtles. To my delight, I found - and caught - a baby cottonmouth, which impressed the hell out of Jess and Madison both. Fortunately, I didn't add a third venomous snake bite to my life story that day.

After a while, our time in the forest ended and we went our separate ways. I was left with a feeling I couldn't explain. It was happiness and a feeling of connection that I had yearned for, but it also came with a gut-wrenching sense of dread. What was I doing? I had a wife, 5 kids, a house, and a life I was trying to make simpler, but I couldn't shake this feeling. There was something there.

A week later, Jess and I came back alone, spending our time walking, talking, and cutting our initials into a tree with Jess's knife she always seemed to have. As day turned into night, I started feeling the wear of my boots. With more thoughts on Jess and less on practical footwear, I made the rookie mistake of wearing work boots instead of something to hike in. As I took them off and started walking through the forest barefoot, I could see a small smirk on Jess's face. She laughed and made fun of me, but I could tell she was impressed. There was definitely something there.

It was dark when we finally got back to the car. It was time to go and we both knew it, but neither one of us wanted to say goodbye. We both stood in the middle of a deserted parking lot and turned our eyes to the vast sky filled with stars. I was trying to think of anything that would keep us together just a few minutes longer.

"Look at how many stars there are!", I said.

"They're beautiful!", she said.

I took that chance and laid down on the pavement in hopes she would follow suit. She did. In silence, we stared at the beauty in front of us. Being my brainiac self, I broke the silence by naming off constellations, Orion's Belt being my favorite. She seemed impressed and I kept going. To my surprise, she pulled out a flashlight she had used on our hike, turned it on, and directed it to the sky.

"Where...?" Her voice trailed off. Realizing how stupid she looked aiming her flashlight to the sky, she laughed hysterically. "See, that's how smart I am."

We both laughed, and it was at that moment I realized how much I really liked this girl. And if I had to put my finger on the moment things changed for us, I think it would be that night. I knew she was something special. The only thing that went through my mind was, "Holy fuck, this is my dream girl!"

That night, I texted Erin and told her I was moving out. Thomas offered to let me live with him, his girlfriend, and their two kids.

I felt like things were turning around for me.

I was progressing through the drug court program, which required random drug tests and accountability calls three times a day for eighteen months. Fortunately, as a result of the drug court requirements and trying to start the new business, I was rarely home. I guess I could have spent more time with the kids, but I didn't want to be around Erin, so I didn't even try. Instead, I spent all my free time with Jess.

"Yo, Ben. Ben!", Jess said, bringing my attention back to her. "What are you doing on your phone, playing Trivia Crack?", she teased.

We were cleaning up Thomas's garage because I intended to restart Retech, but I had gotten distracted by some notifications on my phone. I looked up. "No, I just made a sale." I had also restarted a gun e-commerce brand called Black Rifle Co. that was shut down when I went to jail. After getting sober, I resurrected the business using my contact list. It was doing quite well.

She looked shocked. It was probably not the answer she was expecting. "A sale? What do you mean?"

"I just made a $100 sale for my gun parts business." I showed her the marketplace on my phone.

"Wait, what? How does that work?", she asked.

I laughed. "It's drop shipping. I never have to physically possess the actual product. I just fulfill orders." Jess having no past experience with anything e-commerce was still a little puzzled, but she was intrigued.

We started spending a lot more time together, still only friends, but inseparable just the same. Thomas had his own house with Jackie, his girlfriend, and they had an extra room for me. Naturally, with Jess and I spending so much time together, she would stay the night and we would sleep in the same bed, laying on the same Angry Birds pillow and talking until we fell asleep. There was a comfort in knowing I had someone to truly connect with on a deep level without anything physical. That lasted about three weeks until we officially became an item.

Thomas's house was not the best solution to our laundry list of problems, but as long as we were together, we were happy. We did what we could to keep it going, which meant a lot of travel back and forth. I wasn't being the best father and Jess wasn't being the best mother. We were newly clean addicts and the selfishness was still there. The dream for both of us was to make enough money to get a house for everyone to move into, but that didn't seem likely to happen anytime soon. Strangely enough, that dream came true when Erin called me a few weeks after I moved in with Thomas.

"What's up?", I answered.

"I'm done," said Erin. "I can't take this anymore. I need a break, and I need to reset. I'm going to get a job."

"Hey, calm down. What's going on?" She seemed to be in full meltdown mode.

"I'm moving out tomorrow, going to find an apartment. You can keep the house, and the kids are your responsibility now." Then she hung up.

I was stunned.

"What happened?", asked Jess.

I looked at her. "Erin said she's moving out and I need to keep the kids."

I wanted my house back and I wanted my kids even more, but now I had complicated things. What was I going to do about Jess?

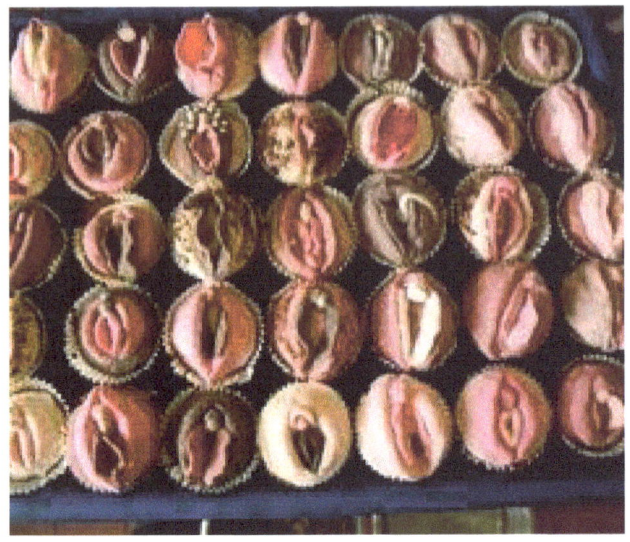

The cupcake picture

The Trio - Thomas, Jessica, and Ben

Jess and the '63 Impala

Ben and Madison (Maddy)

Ben and the baby snake in Shelby Forest

CHAPTER SEVEN
LYING AND CHEATING

JULY 2015

"Come on man, just one drink," said Thomas. "I just got out, and we need to celebrate."

In July, I got drunk with Thomas. He was in drug court as well, and supposed to stay sober, which was why he had been in jail in the first place. It was also one of the reasons we shouldn't have gone drinking when he got out. The other was Jess, who was coming up on one year clean. However, it wasn't just about celebrating with Thomas. When I drank, there was always an underlying reason. Jess didn't know that about me yet. Guilt over a brief affair I'd had with a married woman from NA had triggered my latest relapse. Even worse, Judge Dwyer had specifically ordered me not to have relationships with any women in drug court. The woman's husband had learned about the affair and reported us, so when I went in for a routine piss test, they threw me in jail for contempt of court. Jess thought I had failed the test until the woman's husband sent her a note revealing everything about our affair. When I was released five days later, Jess beat the crap out of me, and I let her. I deserved it. In the end, I was black, blue, and bleeding, and she was crying.

To top it all off, Jess was pregnant.

So, I did the most logical thing that a person in my situation could do, I resolved to get my shit together, something I had done every time Erin had gotten pregnant. I tried to become the man my family needed me to be. Jess had forgiven me—again—and this time, I was determined not to blow it. I needed to straighten up, start doing my twelve step program, and start making money again. And my dedication seemed to pay off from the very beginning.

"So, Retech." Greg was my sponsor at NA, and he approached me one day after a meeting like he usually did, but this time he wanted to talk business. "You've mentioned this company before, and it sounds like you can make some money now that you're sober."

"It would take a significant investment to get it started, Greg. I basically ran it into the ground." I'd had plans to restart, but with all the moving, I hadn't really got around to it. Not to mention I didn't have the money.

"Well, I was thinking I could be a partner and give you some seed cash."

I was over the moon. I knew I could build that business back. Greg was an anesthesiologist. He had the dough to make it happen. It felt like my commitment to sobriety and getting my life back on track was being rewarded with this opportunity. Greg invested the money for the relaunch, and I would provide the expertise and labor. Our deal was that I didn't get any money until the investment was paid back in full.

In no time, we had truckloads of televisions coming into a warehouse I'd rented. I dove in full speed ahead, feeling like I was finally heading in a positive direction. Jess dove in too, pregnant and all, stripping TVs with the best of them. Kids swapping between Erin, myself, and Jess was a regular three-ring circus act, but we managed. And on November 13th, 2015, my 34th birthday, Retech 2.0 had its very first sale.

While the plan to repay the invested money sounded solid at the time, it quickly became untenable. After all, my contribution to the partnership was to do all the work, but I wasn't getting a paycheck. I had bills to pay. I needed an income to provide for myself and my family. The longer I went without one, the more stressed I became.

As the extreme pressures that came with the rapid growth of the business piled on to the financial strain of not bringing home a paycheck, I quickly remembered why Erin had deliberately sabotaged the business in the first place—it was bad for my sobriety. Her words from that fight circled through my head. Running Retech stressed you out so much. The hours you worked were insane. I just want you to be sober, healthy…

As angry as I still sometimes was with her for having made that unilateral decision, I couldn't deny that there had been a healthy dose of wisdom in her words. I might still wish she had gone about it a different way, but she wasn't wrong. However, I ignored the alarm bells going off in my head.

To add to the chaos, Jess and I began growing Black Rifle Co., running both businesses out of the same warehouse. Over Thanksgiving 2015, it went viral, making $7000 that month alone. We were still working hard at Retech for free, hoping that would eventually pay out.

Regardless, our finances were getting back on track and I hadn't relapsed, so we were winning.

In December 2015, I disappeared on a bender for a few days, and she knew me better now. To make matters worse, drug court had put a warrant out on me because I hadn't checked in. Jess was entering her second trimester of pregnancy and was violently ill. The toll of pregnancy, stress, and being clean for the first time since she was 13 weighed heavy on a heart that had just been shattered a few weeks before. She was hurt and understandably so, but she was also well-versed in relapses. Not knowing what to do or who to reach out to, she called my parents.

Jess had never met my parents before this. She had only heard stories about my childhood, but it was very apparent to her that my parents loved me. She bit the bullet and made the call. "Hey, it's Jess. I'm worried about Ben. He's been gone for 3 days and I'm scared he may be in trouble. He calls every once in a while, but he's so out of it, he's not making sense anymore."

My dad flew down the next day and saw me in all of my crack-addled glory. It took a while, but he finally convinced me to come back home. That night was rough and I'm sure it was even rougher on them having to listen to me as I tossed and turned, mumbling and groaning words that didn't seem human. I felt like death and I looked even worse.

The first question from Jess came as soon as I woke up. "Did you cheat again?"

"The court said you cheated with that same woman again."

"But I didn't. She texted me and that's it. I didn't touch her."

While I slept, Jess had scoured my devices with a fine-tooth comb, and in the end, she believed my story.

"Doesn't matter," she told me. "Now we have a different problem. They have a warrant out for you. You're gonna have to turn yourself in, and when you get screened, you're gonna fail."

I started freaking out again. If the judge wanted to be hard on me, I could go to prison for forty years if he sent my case to criminal court and I got convicted of everything I was charged with. I sat on the bed and put my head in my hands. "Fuck. What are we gonna do?" I really wanted more dope in that moment.

"We could replace your urine."

I looked up, not quite sure what I had just heard.

"What? How? With what?"

"We can pick up a catheter at a medical supply store, then use it to replace your pee with mine. I'm sober, so when you pee, it should come back clean." Her love for me had no bounds.

Before I'd met her, Jess had been a Certified Medical Assistant. But having my angry girlfriend jam a tube up my penis sounded like the worst idea in the history of humanity. Unfortunately, I couldn't think of a better one, and I definitely didn't want to go to jail.

"Fine, fuck it."

With our brilliant plan in place, we drove to CAAP for my screen. We wanted to do the procedure as close to the testing facility as possible so that I wouldn't have an opportunity to make my own urine prior to the test. We stopped in a parking lot across the street from the courthouse, then got into the back seat of the truck.

As anyone in their right mind can imagine, it was a disaster from the beginning, and there was piss all over the truck by the time we were finished. I was doubtful that it worked, but it wasn't for a lack of trying. And if the pain was any indication of how much I wanted it to work, then it was going to be a glorious success.

I couldn't even urinate during the screen. I called Bryan and admitted everything. He advised me to throw myself on the mercy of the court.

The following day, I turned myself in and was sentenced to a ten-day sanction in jail, which, given the worst-case scenario, had us both breathing a sigh of relief.

I woke up to a man dressed in scrubs leaning over me. "What denomination are you, son?" asked the doctor.

"What in the fuck are you talking about?", I asked. "Where am I?"

"You're in the jail clinic. You're in kidney failure, you're dying. The ambulance is on its way. We're trying to get a chaplain in here for you, just in case."

I tried to remember what had happened. I'd spent ten miserable days in jail, then was brought before the judge again.

"Mr. Owen, I told you if you fucked me, I'd fuck you back, did I not? I'm terminating you from the drug court program and sending your case to criminal court for prosecution. Bond set at $200,000. Deputy, get him the fuck out of my courtroom."

My heart sank. There was absolutely no way I could pay that. I hadn't even been able to contact Jess, because as soon as I got to my pod, I started feeling sick. The guards thought I was faking it and ignored me.

"You have a fever of 108," the jail doctor continued, "and you have some kind of infection."

The ambulance drove me to the hospital, and I was immediately put into the ICU. They diagnosed me with Pyelonephritis, probably caused by the catheter incident. I was in acute renal failure and had sepsis. For five days, I stayed in the intensive care unit on the verge of death.

When they finally allowed me to call Jess on the day before Christmas, my voice was hoarse because I'd been intubated. "I'm in the ICU. I'm in renal failure and they think I'm dying."

"Oh my God!", said Jess.

I continued to blubber through everything that had happened. I'm not even sure she understood. "I'm shackled to the bed. I don't want to die alone." Then, they took the phone away from me.

A couple of weeks later, my condition had improved enough for me to be dragged back to jail, and my attorney had fast-tracked both my indictment and a bond reduction hearing. Jess, Erin, and my dad went before the judge on my behalf to appeal my case, pleading for mercy since I was the only breadwinner for the kids. The criminal court judge lowered the bond to eighty thousand dollars, which was still well outside our reach.

Afterward, I called Erin first. I had some time to think, and she was important to the only plan I could think of. Then I called Jess.

"I know this is going to be awkward as fuck," I told her. "You don't like Erin much, but I have a plan to get me out of jail. Erin's going to be coming over, and y'all are going to have to figure this out together. She knows the business. We need to start selling things: the gun safe, ammo, stocks, whatever we can to get me out of here. Erin knows where everything is and how to sell it."

It was a big ask. Jess was already watching the kids when Erin went to work, so they were at least talking every day, but I knew there was tension. How could there not be after what I'd put them both through?

Hearing my parents testify on my behalf about the dangers of kidney shutdown due to drugs and their appeal to the judge to lessen my bond really messed with my head. Once again, I saw how my choices were seriously affecting the mental health of the ones I loved. I felt like a selfish piece of shit.

I had no hope that Erin would be able to come up with the money, even when I suggested the guns and equipment. I even told her to look into getting a second mortgage on the house, but we were so behind on payments that it didn't even seem possible. Then, after sixty days, I heard my name called.

"Owen, pack your shit, you made bond."

I was told I had to go across the street to sign some paperwork. I didn't know how Erin did it, but she got the bonding company to accept our deed to a house that was on its way into foreclosure as collateral on my bond. After completing all the documents, I called her and she picked me up; Jess had the kids. About halfway home, she asked, "You called her first, didn't you?"

The question caught me off guard. I thought I'd been clear that I wanted the divorce, and I thought Erin wanted it, too. Sure, she scrambled to get me out of jail, but that was just so I could provide for the kids, wasn't it?

"I called Jess, yeah."

The pain in her expression made it clear how badly I'd misread the situation. Erin wasn't just fighting for our kids; she was still fighting for us.

We reached the intersection on the drive home where Erin would need to turn one way to take me to Jess or the other direction to head to her new place. She stopped at the crossroads and paused for a few seconds.

"Which way?" she asked quietly.

Erin. The mother of my five children. The woman who had stayed with me throughout everything.

"Please, take me home to Jess. I'm sorry, Erin." To this day, those were the hardest words I ever had to say to anyone. To this very day.

But I knew they were the right ones, for both of us.

Back home with Jess again, I worked hard to support my family and stay sober, but that only lasted for five more months.

Jess, pregnant with James

Jacob (age 10) working at Retech

Getting Retech ready - pallets of broken TVs

CHAPTER EIGHT
THE ROLLERCOASTER

MAY 2016

I chose Jessica, but I still couldn't get my act together.

On May 17, 2016, I relapsed on crack just after Jess gave birth to James. She hadn't even been released from the hospital. I thought I was hiding it from her, but later found out that she knew, she just chose to stay quiet. She was tired, in pain, and didn't want to risk the possibility that the doctor might take our baby away. Additionally, she realized that the guilt from that relapse might put me in yet another spiral. She kept her mouth shut for the sake of our family, and we headed home with James...and a prescription for percocet.

We had gotten Black Rifle Co up and running again after I was released from jail, but I was no longer part of Retech; Greg and I parted ways during my incarceration, and he eventually sold the company. Money was coming in, but we were just breaking even on our bills, and with the new baby, I was stressed beyond belief with my responsibilities to support my family.

Outwardly, things appeared to be going well for the next three weeks. Unfortunately, I couldn't stop the series of relapses that had begun. In June, I headed to Woodward Street to buy crack and was arrested by Memphis Organized Crime Unit in a sting operation. I served thirty days waiting for a court date, and the judge finally let me go with time served. Jess was furious when I got home. Fortunately, she was able to keep Black Rifle Co afloat while I was gone. I stayed sober for the next five months, and by November 2017, the company was doing well enough that we were able to start getting out from under our mountain of debt. Finally, we had some space to breathe.

Our mortgage hadn't been paid for the two years Jess and I had been together, on top of the two years I hadn't paid when I'd still been with Erin. I'd been focusing on paying everything else, and the bank foreclosed on the house in March 2017. When I was notified, I couldn't handle it. It was the place where I had lived through so much, where three of my children had been born, and where I founded my businesses. It was like we couldn't catch a break. The debt felt insurmountable, so I'd decided to ignore it instead of dealing with it. I honestly thought my family was going to end up in the street. I disappeared on Jessica, falling down a hole of drinking for a few days until I finally came back with my tail between my legs.

Luckily Jess had made a deal with the new owners of ReTech and we were able to get a check for $7,000. I was so lost that I was ready to let the business go for nothing, but Jess had put too much blood, sweat, and tears into that business and wasn't going to leave empty-handed. In May 2017, we used that money as a security deposit for a new, bigger house, one that would be ours.

The fear of being homeless with my family caused me to continue drinking. There was no hiding it, often leaving for days at a time on a bender. Jessica preferred I not come home because she didn't want the kids to see me like that. She was still on pills, which made her a little mean, but she got a lot done; they gave her energy. She managed to keep the businesses running, the house clean, and the kids fed.

Realizing how bad my drinking had gotten, Jess and I came up with a plan for me to get a shot called Vivitrol, which was supposed to block the good feeling that comes with drinking. What we didn't realize was that it would make me extremely violent when I did drink. Jess finally insisted in June 2017 that I move out in order to protect the kids and herself. So, I moved back in with Thomas.

After a week, I needed clothes. "I'm coming to grab some shit." I was angry that I had once again been kicked out of another house I owned.

"Fine," Jess replied. She wasn't happy with the situation either, I made it to the house and went inside to see James. Thomas came in with me to assess the situation and once he realized how tense things were getting, he had James follow him outside to the truck.

"I'm just coming to get my shit," I told her again.

"Of course you are, so you can fucking leave like you always do!"

I got in her face

"I don't want to be anywhere near you," I said as meanly as I could.

She shoved me. "Get the fuck outta my face!"

After that, all I remember was blood being everywhere. On the walls, on my clothes, on the floor, and pouring from my arm. I found out later that when she pushed me, I snapped. Then, I bashed her head into the wall so bad she almost blacked out. Jess was a survivor though, and she did what Jess does--pulled out her knife and slashed the shit out of my arm. After wrestling for the knife, Jess made a break for the bedroom, where I caught her and began choking her. Consumed with rage, Vivitrol, and alcohol, I had tried to kill my best friend.

Luckily, Thomas heard what was going on from the driveway and rushed into the bedroom where Jess was starting to lose consciousness. He pulled me off of her and took me to the truck.

"Jess, I just had a heart attack." I said shakily through the phone

"What the fuck, Ben?!" There was a concern in her voice, but there was still a lot of anger.

Six days after I almost killed Jess, I was lying in a hospital, in alcohol withdrawal, and had just had a heart attack. I didn't want to live like this anymore. I wanted my life back.

I decided to make some changes and once the doctors cleared me, I walked through the doors of Delta Medical for detox. I got sober and after I was released in August 2017, I apologized to Jess.

Unfortunately, my relapse caught the attention of my probation officer and resulted in him issuing a violation and a warrant for my arrest. Shelby County Sheriff's Deputies showed up at our house to serve it. I ran, and a manhunt with canines ensued.

It took them hours to finally catch me, then I was thrown back into jail. Judge Coffee had a reputation for being a no-nonsense judge, but to the amazement of not only the prosecution, but even my defense attorney, he sentenced me to time served and disposed of the case I'd spent the last three years dealing with. He was strict, but fair, and he understood that I was an addict trying my best to get back on track, not a violent criminal. In the end, he didn't see any public benefit in sending me to prison. I was free and clear, with no legal supervision, no paper, nothing - and I wasn't a felon. That entire debacle with fourteen felony charges was reduced to two misdemeanors for simple possession of a controlled substance.

After that, I was clean and grateful as hell to be out of jail. We got Black Rifle Co back on its feet. Everything seemed to be turning around for us, but there was one more thing.

"Hey Ben," Jess said one night in October from our huge bathtub, relaxing from pressures of the day. "Will you marry me?"

I froze in the closet. I didn't even remember what I was looking for. Walking back into the center of the bathroom, I smiled. "Seriously?" I'd proposed to her at least four times over the last year.

"Yeah. I wanna get married."

I whooped and jumped in the bath with her, soaking the floor. "What changed your mind?"

"Well," she said. "I just want to marry my best friend and spend the rest of my life with him."

We picked out a ring almost immediately, but didn't make any other immediate plans. Suddenly, Black Rifle Co began selling like crazy and we were seriously low on free time. Jessica wasn't the traditional type; she didn't care about a big wedding. Her focus, like mine, was on work. We knew we would make it official one day and that was good enough for both of us. Before we knew it, three months had passed.

"Let's get married now, no more waiting. I've never understood women who wait a year to get married all so they can make it look good for everyone else. This is for us. Let's just do it."

I smiled. "Let's do it."

"So, what do we do next? I have no idea."

"Find someone to ordain the marriage."

Jess hopped on Google and found someone, then agreed on a location and a date.

"February 7th at Starbucks at Union and Mclean," she told me.

"What? Seriously?"

"I mean, I like coffee."

I was going to marry my best friend at a Starbucks.

"Ben! We're actually getting fucking married!" She wrapped her arms around me in excitement. We had endured one hell of a past together and now we were both looking forward to what the future held for us.

As excited as I was, I felt a tug within me. I didn't want her to ever regret her decision to move so quickly.

"Jess" I looked deep into her eyes "Are you sure this is what you want? I mean, like this? To get married at a Starbucks?"

"I am," she told me. "I just want to marry my best friend. Plus, if we're gonna spend a shitload of money, it better be on the honeymoon. Weddings are stupid. They're for everyone else."

A few days later, we were wed at Starbucks. A barista and a random person sipping coffee signed as witnesses. We were officially Mr. and Mrs. Ben Owen.

That was one of the happiest moments of my life—just in time, too. Because bad times were soon to follow.

"Baby, we've got like five thousand dollars leaving our bank account each month." I was calm and in no way accusatory.

"It can't be that much," she insisted.

I showed her the bank withdrawals. She had been buying the pills from her sister and lost track of everything we were spending. I apologized again for all the ways I had let her down, but this had to be addressed.

"It's ok, I get it, but baby, we can't keep this up," I told her. "We've gotta figure out how to start weaning you off."

She agreed, and we made a plan to slowly cut back. I had so much guilt. She was resentful for all the time I'd spent in jail and all the time she'd had to raise the kids alone, trying to keep the business afloat while I refused to face my responsibilities. I knew I had to take the lead to get us out of this hole.

It was tough. Orders came in nonstop, and she took pills to stay normal and productive. On our record day, we sold over $41,000 of product. But I started getting nervous because our sales volume was skyrocketing, and our customer service was going down the tube. I was also concerned about the underwriting for our credit card sales, but our sales rep assured us everything was fine. So, we kept selling. Jess was a machine and worked just like I did. I not only had a thriving business, but I had also finally found someone who could match my work ethic.

During the next month, we barely made a dent in her pill consumption. Then, in March, an apparent "drought" hit the illicit pill supply chain in Memphis - we couldn't find her pills ANYWHERE. Jess became violently dope-sick, and it broke my heart to see her like that. I let it go on for about a day before finally breaking down and going to get her some heroin. It was the only thing I could do to make her well. That would turn out to be one of the worst decisions I would ever make.

With Jess doing heroin, it was really hard to keep my mind off of it. I wanted it too. Pills I could do without, but heroin was a different story. About a week later I started shooting up. We soon developed a thirty thousand dollars a month drug habit, but with the success of the company, we could afford it.

Within a month or two, we were selling over half a million dollars a month, and our credit card processors suddenly froze our payouts. Our sudden growth was too much of a red flag. We weren't doing anything wrong, but our success had caused a risk investigation by the underwriting bank. With all our money in limbo, we couldn't pay any of our bills, our distributors, or our shipping company.

Now, we couldn't afford our drug habits. Our house was stuffed with inventory that we couldn't move. Things started to spiral fast from that moment.

The credit card companies informed us they would hold most of our money until the investigation was over. We were forced to give refunds to all the clients since the payments didn't go through, and each disputed purchase came with a twenty-five-dollar fee. We began selling our inventory wholesale to pay for our drug habit, losing money with every transaction. It was rough. Every day, I told myself it would be the last hit. After every hit, I'd say, *I'm gonna change tomorrow.*

About a month into making runs back and forth to Woodward Street, I had gotten back on crack. We were both still doing heroin, but I was an overachiever. One day Jess woke up very dope-sick and we were out of heroin.

"All I have is crack," I told her

"I'm so fucking sick. I hurt everywhere. I feel like I'm dying."

I hated seeing her sick, which just made me want to do drugs to forget. I added crack to my shooter and got ready to hit it, then looked at her. She had her hand out, and I handed the pipe to her.

Putting it to her mouth, she asked, "How bad of an idea would it be for me to hit this."

"It will be the worst decision you will ever make," I told her.

She paused for about three seconds. "Fuck it."

Jess had now smoked crack for the first time.

Now, crack consumed even more money, and we were running out. We were still chemically dependent on heroin and decided to go to an out-patient methadone clinic, willing to try anything to stop. Our plan was to be on methadone for two months, just in time for Christmas. It didn't exactly work that way.

We'd stop by the clinic around 5 am to get our methadone, then stop by the trap house on the way back to pick up crack. We never completed the methadone clinic, though we did eventually wean ourselves off heroin. Unfortunately, crack was a much bigger monster and it consumed every bit of our lives. Things continued to go downhill at an accelerated pace. By Christmas we were full blown crack addicts. Nothing mattered anymore: not the bills, the house, our children, nothing. On Christmas day, we were smoking crack on Woodward Street.

"Yo, whatchall even doing here?", one of the dope boys asked.

"We're smoking," I told him.

"Naw mane, ain't you gotta be home for Christmas? Ain't you got kids?"

Shit. The guilt hit us like a freight train. There was no Christmas tree and the only presents we had for the kids were a few that my mom had sent. We had been so consumed in getting our next high we'd completely forgotten all about it.

"Ben, there are 3 huge guys here to evict us," Jess told me on the phone. "They're throwing all of our shit out because we're behind on our rent."

"What the fuck?" I had been on a drug run when the truck suddenly stopped running. "The truck finally shit the bed for good. I'm supposed to be meeting with a guy right now to sell it. I'll be there as soon as I can." I had found a website that would buy my 2008 Z71 Tahoe for $1,500, no questions asked. They sent a tow truck to pick it up, and the driver would have my check. The truck was easily worth six times that, but I was too desperate to care.

"Ben?" asked Jessica.

"Yeah?"

"Get some shit while you're out"

Luckily Madison was out of town on a trip so she didn't have to witness what was going on. James was two and I'm sure he knew something was wrong but he was content playing with his toys.

I got home about an hour later to see half of our belongings already sitting on the front lawn. The gravity of what was happening hit a little harder seeing it happen in real time. I had failed again. To make matters worse, it was pouring down rain.

Jess's dad got us a U-Haul and we fit what we could in it. To add insult to injury, at that moment, it started sleeting. God was angry and the sleet was just an added punishment. We dropped James off with Jessica's dad and headed to the trap house, where we stayed for five days smoking our cares away with the last of our money.

Jess's dad, Jay, allowed us to stay on a mattress on the living room floor when we were home. He obviously knew something was going on but allowed us to come and go as we pleased. The disappointment was apparent. I'm sure he felt helpless and didn't know what to do or say. We knew we were burning the last of our bridges, but the pull of addiction was just too strong. By February 7, 2019, we had gone from successful and swimming in money, to broke and destitute crack addicts spending our first wedding anniversary on Jay's floor, three feet away from where Jess's mom had overdosed and died 15 years prior.

Between February and May, we bounced from living in a $700 truck we managed to buy, to living in Jay's house, to detox, to living in trap houses. This was not the life we wanted. Although we had become full blown addicts, we had never lost our faith in God. Every time we reached some level of sobriety or awareness, we would say the same prayer. "God, if you will get us out of this hell together, we promise we will come back for those we leave behind." Sometimes we would say it in the trap house on Woodward, sitting on plywood floors. Sometimes it would be said in our truck as we aimlessly drove around looking for our next fix. Sometimes we would pray it with tears streaming down our faces after another friend had left this Earth too soon. Sometimes we would be getting high while we prayed it. Regardless, we always meant every single word.

My mom decided to take James for about a week, which allowed us to detox. We didn't go to rehab, there was no time, but we had finally had enough. Everyone we knew in Memphis was dying or getting locked up, and the walls felt like they were caving in around us. We got out of detox determined to do right, excited about starting life over again, clean. Then, tragedy struck again.

"Jess, Nick might have been murdered. We're trying to find out more."

Nick was Madison's father. He and Jess had been friends since they were 12 and had been in a relationship on and off for 10 years before he went to prison and Jess went into rehab. He had his issues. He was also an addict and alcoholic, and had been in and out of prison since I had known him. Once he found out Jess and I were together, he didn't like it but respected the way I was able to care for his daughter. He would later ask for advice on things, and, in a weird way, I'd become a mentor to him.

He'd finally gotten out of prison and was hell bent on getting his act together and having Maddy for the summer. I had convinced him to move to Alabama, where the majority of his family lived. He did, and he worked hard enough to get his own trailer. We were about to allow Maddy to stay with him for the summer, but I told him that his addict roommate needed to go. Nick told his roommate to move out, ecstatic that he would finally have time with Maddy.

I was on the phone seconds before he died, talking to him about Maddy's arrival.

"I'm painting her room right now," he told me. "I can't wait to see her." The happiness in his voice was palpable

"I'm proud of you, man. You really did good."

"Hey, someone's at the door, hold on, Ima call you back."

Those were the last words I would ever hear from Nick. His roommate, high on meth, murdered him that night.

Jess was a sobbing mess, I was riddled with guilt, blaming myself for having Nick kick out his roommate. We came back that afternoon, high on crack, and sadly broke the news to Maddy. I began to drink heavily again. The guilt consumed me and I just wanted an escape. We were both right back where we started: hopelessly addicted and going nowhere fast.

The next month was a blur. In and out of blackouts, being held at gunpoint, getting kidnapped with Jess and James. This life had become completely unmanageable and I wanted to die. In the haze that was our life, needing more crack and alcohol, I stole Jess's phone and ran, leaving her in the truck with James. I went off the deep end for a few weeks, barely remembering anything, until I woke up barefoot in front of 1428 Woodward Street. Then, I made the choice that changed my life.

    I chose my family and my future and walked away from the dope. Just taking that step in the right direction made all the difference.

Ben and James 5/17/2016

The new house - after the foreclosure of Ben and Erin's house.

Ben's mugshot - 3 weeks after James's birth.

One big happy family (Jess was on pills- opiates)

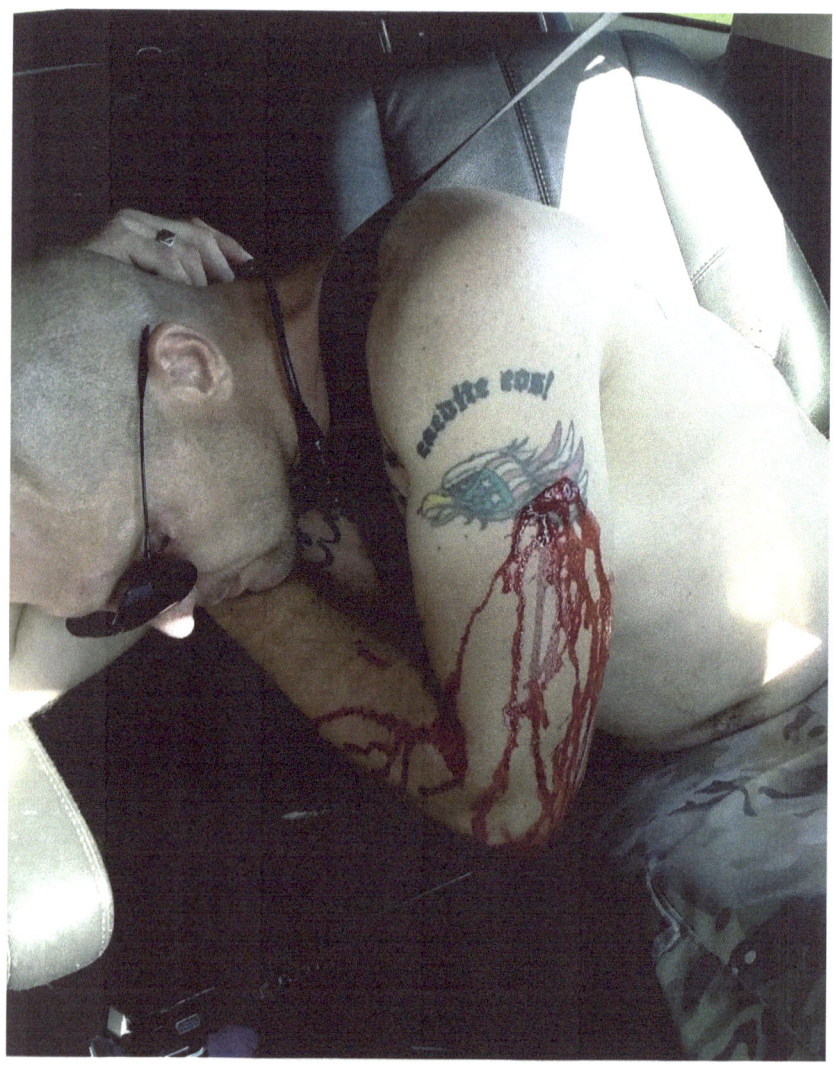

Ben's knife wound from Jess

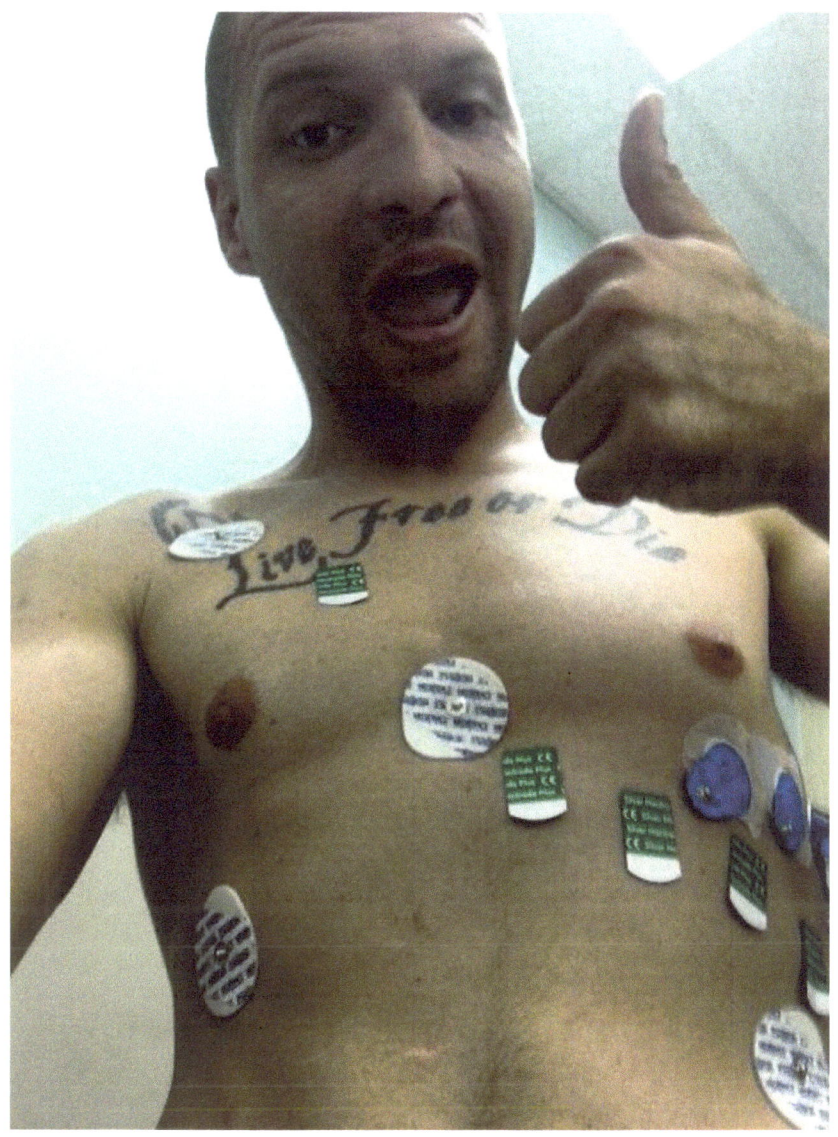

Ben after his heart attack (very drunk)

BEN OWEN & JESSICA OWEN

This is the only picture we have from the night we were married at Starbucks 2/7/2018 (Jess was on pills - opiates)

The eviction 1/5/2019

Nick and Madison

CHAPTER NINE
GOD WORKS IN MYSTERIOUS WAYS

MAY 2019

AT THE BUS STATION, I CALLED JESS AND LAID OUT MY PLAN. I'd finally had enough.

"I'm leaving," I told her. "I'm going to my parents' house. We'll figure out what to do with James later."

"Whatever, man."

"I'll be here when you're ready, or I won't, it's up to you." I hung up knowing it was the right decision.

A week later Jess called for me to come get her. She had hit her end and was done too. She had the truck, but I had stupidly taken the keys with me when I went to Atlanta, so back on a greyhound bus I went, straight back to Memphis, to get my wife and child.

We packed up everything we owned in garbage bags, loaded down the truck, and headed away from Memphis.

"Slow down just a little," I told Jess, who was driving.

I held my camera steady and aimed it at the rearview mirror and took a picture.

I posted it on Facebook with the caption, *Goodbye Memphis, we're leaving this motherfucker behind for good!* We had finally done it. We had left hell. Together.

We drove on for about 20 minutes. We were scared, but felt hope and relief take over us. No way should we even be alive, much less getting out of Memphis.

"We gotta go back."

What? Why? Did you leave something?"

"No," I said, "We have work to do in Memphis. Maybe not right now, but I feel like we're supposed to go back."

"Yeah, okay." Jess said and we both busted out in laughter

I needed to feel like I didn't have choices. Choices would make it too easy not to get up in the morning, too easy to relax in the moment, and too easy to fall back into the world of addiction.

I couldn't let that happen.

So, when I finally brought Jess and James back from Memphis to live with my parents, they slept on twin beds upstairs in the guest room and I stayed on the couch, despite my parents offering to buy me a bed. My family needed me, and being comfortable wouldn't motivate me to get up every morning and hustle. I knew myself, knew I needed to want things to get better or this wouldn't work.

For two months, I worked odd jobs on Fiverr and Upwork, offering e-commerce mentoring for peanuts and only making $1000 during that whole time, but every dollar in my pocket got me closer to helping my family.

Then, a guy named Howard messaged me on Upwork. "Hey, you seem to have quite a background. Tell me about yourself."

We messaged back and forth about my experience until he finally wanted to talk on the phone. I was in Best Buy purchasing a new mouse when he called me with a proposal that was too good to be true, especially after everything we'd been through.

He had ten e-commerce brands that he needed help promoting through Google ads, Facebook ads, email marketing, and other platforms. The job he offered me paid through revenue sharing, which meant the more I worked, the more money I would make, and I was fine with that. Though he didn't promise anything, he made it seem like I could be averaging ten thousand dollars a month in no time. As recovering addicts, Jessica and I were used to false promises, and we were always on our guard. But Howard talked a good game, and if he delivered on even half of what he was saying, it would improve our situation. Anyway, I wasn't looking for a long-term job. I just wanted to get back on my feet so I could create my own business again. While the job seemed like pie in the sky, it also sounded like it would at least get us out of my parents' house quicker.

I showed up at Howard's office dressed to impress in the only suit I'd brought from Memphis. There was a blue Lamborghini Gallardo parked outside with a vanity plate that read "Click Me". *Subtle,* I thought. The building was impressive too, lots of employees and really expensive decor. I later found out the fossilized mammoth tusk on the wall cost over a hundred grand.

When we sat down to talk, I realized he was pulling a bait and switch. While he did have the e-commerce websites he had mentioned, there was no inventory. He was drop-shipping from China and had lied his ass off just to get me in the office. And he didn't bring me to handle that part of his business. Instead, he wanted me to help sell the services from two other businesses he owned. The first was a consumer marketing company called Alligatr, and the second was a data business-to-business company called Clickme, which could make predictions about what a particular device user might be about to spend money on. I was fascinated by what he said those companies were capable of. The capabilities of this system to market products and services to a specific group of individuals had incredibly lucrative possibilities, but Howard was unsure how to monetize it in a B2C way at scale.

My immediate thoughts were how I might use this to improve Black Rifle Co, and no matter what else happened in my relationship with Howard—which, granted, had begun on a bed of lies—I was determined to look under the hood and figure out how to optimize Clickme for my own uses.

Howard brought me onboard to help get the Alligatr startup off the ground since it hadn't made even one sale yet. The potential for this was so huge. To be honest, I would have paid to get the information if he had asked—and if I'd had any money. Regardless, my hustle was back in a big way.

The job was perfect for my skill set. Plus, it was only a thirty-minute drive from my parents' house, and I even got a key card, which made me feel fancy. I was confident that I would be making money soon.

I started busting my ass for him. It sucked that Howard was six years younger than me. I hadn't had a boss in over ten years, and I'd never had one so young. He was also extremely difficult to work with, spying on his employees by using hidden cameras and computer tracking software. But I was learning the ropes of data intelligence, and the wheels in my mind were turning to apply the same tactics to firearms consumers.

Robert, the sales manager and lead trainer, was my direct boss. I quickly got several sales, which were the first sales of the company, but it became immediately clear that he had an issue with me. I tried to explain that he was using outdated training models, but this just seemed to cause more tension between us. I worked on company marketing and client ads, doing $10,000 worth of business for the company over the next two months, while only receiving about $1,500 a month for my trouble. I was supposed to be getting paid a commission on the sales, but the money came in slower than I had expected, and Howard wasn't completely trustworthy.

Finally, after three months, I started making $2,500 a month. Despite being glad to receive a paycheck, I didn't feel my compensation lined up with the number of accounts and amount of money I was bringing in for Howard.

By the end of the year, after working for Howard for five months and only making a total of $7,000, I was miserable. I was working ten hours a day building his business, and I knew I wasn't being paid my worth. My parents and Jess almost convinced me to quit. They were confident I could find a better-paying job somewhere else with my skills and experience. Still, something—God or intuition—told me to stay a little longer. I wasn't at Clickme to make a living, I knew it was bigger than a paycheck. I felt like I would learn something that would change my life.

"No," I told them. "There's something here. I don't know exactly what yet. I don't know if it will help with Black Rifle Co or some new business venture, but there's something here. I just need to figure it out. Be patient. Don't rush it."

Hopefully, I was right, because the stress of the working conditions was significantly damaging my mental health.

"Please check on him," I begged the police officer over the phone. "I haven't heard from him in almost a week, and I feel like something bad has happened. Just do a wellness check. Please." It was December 12th.

The Memphis Narcotics Police Division called me back thirty minutes later; they'd found Brandon Kelly's decomposing body in his apartment. I was gutted. I'd known he'd relapsed, but keeping my distance and protecting my sobriety had seemed like the most responsible thing to do for both me and my family. Sending Erin money so she could bring him food and check in on him was all I'd been willing to risk. In the end, I hadn't been there for him.

I went to the office the next day in a daze. Howard had no sympathy. Vacation days weren't part of my contract. Robert, on the other hand, was an empathetic ear. We had become close over the last few months. He'd even come over to my parent's house for Thanksgiving. He went to bat for me with Howard, convincing him I needed a week off to settle this matter or my head wouldn't be in the right space to help the business.

People in recovery are familiar with the concept of "reservations", a situation or circumstance that you park in the back of your mind when you get clean: "when X happens, I will get high over it." It's a very common thought process for addicts in early recovery, it eases the magnitude of accepting "I can never get high again" if you predefine a scenario in which you get "a pass." For Jess and I, Brandon's death was that reservation we latched onto when we left the streets, we KNEW it was going to happen. Yet, when the moment came, something snapped in our heads, and a relapse wasn't even a consideration. You couldn't have forced us to get high, it wasn't happening. We were done, totally and completely. We just wanted to bury our friend.

Brandon had no family, and he deserved better than whatever burial the county would provide. I reached back out to the Memphis Drug Court and the recovery community who had rightfully written me off as dead. Just as I had distanced myself from Brandon, they had distanced themselves from me. As far as they were concerned, I was toxic. Despite that, when I explained Brandon's situation, they were there with open arms, asking how they could help. Brandon had been in drug court with me, and while I was a failure, Brandon did well with structure and graduated the program with flying colors.

He'd wanted to be cremated and have his ashes scattered in a few different places. The cost was $900, which felt like an insurmountable number at the time. I had three mouths to feed and had only made $7,000 in the last five months. My social media platforms for my various businesses, however, had garnered close to a million followers over the years, so on December 19, 2019, I started a fundraiser to take care of my friend's remains. I ended up receiving over $3,500 in donations. I was so moved by the generosity of people. It was a different side of things I hadn't experienced before.

Jess and I were scared to death on our drive from Atlanta back to Memphis, we both had panic attacks. The whole seven-hour drive there, I white-knuckled the steering wheel, and the only thing I could think about was, *I don't want to fucking do this*. It was terrifying, and we feared a relapse. Being in Georgia, away from everything, made it easy, but going back to the place that had almost taken everything from us was gut wrenching. When we made it there, we said a prayer, wiped our tears, and slowly made our way to the memorial. Candles were lit and a circle of mourners shared stories about our beautiful friend. We ran into people that we hadn't seen in years. People that had written us off, people that had been praying for us, and people that thought we were dead. In Brandon's last act, he had brought us all back together.

After taking care of Brandon's body, I donated the remainder of the money to the Shelby County Drug Court Foundation. $3,500 would have made a huge difference to my family at that point in our lives but it wasn't raised for me, and donating it felt like the right thing to do. That donation changed people's attitudes about us, we weren't just ex-junkies to them anymore. Ultimately, it was a spark for Jessica and me. We realized that the process of raising this money for a good cause had really inspired us.

"I wish we could do this more," I told Jessica as we drove home to Atlanta. "We obviously haven't completely destroyed our relationships with the recovery community in Memphis. Even drug court is open to the possibility that I'm not a piece of shit." I guided the car onto the interstate. "We could help vets battling opiate addiction, often fueled by VA prescriptions. People like Brandon Deaton."

"Maybe someday," said Jessica. "We just have to make sure we're ready to do it for the long haul. Not like before when we had the idea, and then we both relapsed. That wouldn't be fair to those we're trying to help, you know?"

I nodded.

"What was the name you came up with again?", asked Jessica.

"Flanders Fields."

"How does the poem go?"

My eyes misted over as I recited it to her.

> *In Flanders fields, the poppies blow*
> *Between the crosses, row on row,*
> *That mark our place; and in the sky*
> *The larks, still bravely singing, fly*
> *Scarce heard amid the guns below.*
>
> *We are the Dead. Short days ago*
> *We lived, felt dawn, saw sunset glow,*
> *Loved and were loved, and now we lie,*
> *In Flanders fields.*
>
> *Take up our quarrel with the foe:*
> *To you from failing hands we throw*
> *The torch; be yours to hold it high.*
> *If ye break faith with us who die*

We shall not sleep, though poppies grow
In Flanders fields.

We both sat in silence for a few seconds.
"It's a good name," said Jessica.
I sighed. "Maybe someday we'll be able to make it a reality."

Back in Atlanta, my financial situation wasn't getting any better. I think Howard saw everyone as replaceable, except he was wrong in my case. He also thought that I couldn't leave because I needed the little money he was paying and couldn't get another job; again, wrong, because I didn't want to work for anyone. I wanted to work for myself.

Eventually, I learned Robert was afraid I was after his job, which couldn't have been further from the truth. I didn't want to work for anyone; I just wanted to learn what I could use in my own business and split. It wasn't until we shared a beer one night—my last beer ever, which Robert often makes a point of reminding me—that we came to an understanding. That night, we truly bonded. I told him everything, and Robert shared that he'd once had a drinking problem too. I also told him about Jess and my dream to start Flanders Fields to help vets, and he told me of his idea to start a T-shirt company that would also help homeless vets. Once we realized we weren't in competition, we became the best of friends, and Howard became our common enemy. We knew the only way either of us would ever realize our dreams was if we managed to break free from him. Robert started helping me use the Clickme software to analyze my gun part email list, and we got amazing results. I wasn't making money, but the information I gained helped me make a plan for the future.

By the end of January, Robert was trying hard to push me out of the door. I thought he just wanted to help me, but I later learned that he wanted me to succeed so I could create a job for him. He couldn't wait to escape working for Howard either. Still, it was a hard decision because we found out that Jessica was pregnant on January 29th. But I knew it was the right direction for us.

The following week, I finally quit and began brokering deals between Black Rifle Co and some firearm companies. Funnily enough, I became a client of Clickme, using their data collection capabilities in the firearm industry. Instead of selling gun parts, I began selling data to the gun companies, and the business took off immediately.

A month later, we were finally making enough money to move the family into a townhouse of our own.

Two months later, the new owners of ReTech called me to see if I wanted my business back.

"Guess who just called?", I asked Jessica.

"Who?"

"Ben Taube, the guy who bought ReTech from Greg."

"What does that fucker want?"

"He wants to give us ReTech back."

"Are you shitting me? How much does he want?"

"We just take over. If we're able to help them clear some of their credit card debt, they'll look at it as an overall win."

She couldn't believe it.

The new owners had run the business into the ground and were $25,000 in debt, but there was no way that we could look at that and say God wasn't behind everything, pulling the strings. I had restarted that business successfully three times already, and I knew I could do it again.

We rented a 1,500 square foot warehouse, hired some of my fellow AA members to get it started, and used the office space in the warehouse as an office for Black Rifle Co. We made it into a family business, with Jessica and fifteen-year-old Jacob breaking down TVs and teaching recovering alcoholics how to do it while I ran Black Rifle Co and did some logistics work for Retech. We soon had racks stacked twenty feet to the ceiling of TV parts and had maxed out capacity.

COVID helped both businesses in a big way. Everyone wanted to have their TVs working during the pandemic, and delivery was the way to go. As far as Black Rifle Co went, the gun industry was twenty years behind the time, and COVID brought them into the digital age, which was fine with us.

In July, I realized that ReTech had $6,000 held in its Amazon account. I'd had that problem before, and I knew how to release it, but it was an asset that belonged to the previous owners. I called them up and told them about the money.

"Hey man, it's your money, but it would really help me grow the business," I told them.

Unfortunately, they had just got a huge IRS bill and needed the money, but they forgave the $25,000 debt that was loaded on their American Express for my honesty. God works in mysterious ways, that's for sure.

That change gave Black Rifle Co wings, and it started making more money than Retech. A few months later, Robert joined as my partner.

In March 2020, Jessica and I decided we wanted to not only get back into church, but we wanted to join a small group as well, something we had never done together. We met Kelly and Derrick Pittman who were the leaders and hosted meetings at their house. It was a beautiful house, about 4,500 square feet. When we got there, we felt so out of place. All the other members of the group were pulling up in their new vehicles, clean and flawless. We pulled up in our $700 truck, dirty, squeaky, and full of dents. It was embarrassing, but we knew this was where we were supposed to be. We just sat there for a minute to get our bearings. We were so out of our league and we knew it.

As we sat in the basement living room surrounded by people living a life of plenty we'd long ago lost, I had the strangest sensation come over me. It was oddly similar to that Memphis rear view mirror moment; I leaned over to Jess and whispered to her, "I got the weirdest feeling that this house is going to be ours one day."

She looked at me. "You're fucking crazy," she whispered back.

Crazy or not, a year later, the Pittmans were dealing with a lot of issues, and Derrick called to ask if I wanted to lease-purchase the house, which was just insane because there was no way any bank would give me a mortgage with my credit history. But the lease-purchase from the Pittmans was doable, and we moved the whole family in by the end of March.

In April, Brandon Deaton was in serious trouble.

Deaton had lived with Erin and I back in 2012 and was now addicted to pain meds again. We had stayed connected all this time, even though Jessica and I were clean now. On social media, his parents saw everything we were able to accomplish helping Brandon Kelly in Memphis, and they reached out to me hoping I could get Deaton out of a jam.

He was facing a situation similar to what I had faced in 2014—addicted to dope and potentially facing gun charges. I could relate. Jess and I immediately started researching places that could take him, ultimately finding one with space in Texas. But no one had the $2,500 necessary to get him to a rehab center.

I mentioned this situation to Robert, who had become a mentor of sorts on a lot of different things. I often ran large purchases by him for a sanity check.

"Do you see any reason that Black Rifle Co can't fund that rehab just as a good deed?" I asked him.

"Nope. While we're on the topic, whatever happened to your Flanders Fields idea? This would be a perfect justification for doing that."

"Yeah, but we need to do this now."

"Maybe so, but what about the next time, and the time after that? This isn't going to be the last time something like this pops up. Just get the paperwork out of the way, dude."

"I have to focus on Deaton. Anyway, I don't even know how to file for that."

Robert smiled. "That's never stopped you before. All you ever do is shit you don't know how to do, and you keep doing it until you know how to do it better than anybody else."

He was right, of course. But Deaton came first.

It turned out that Sarah Verardo at Independence Fund, another non-profit, stepped in to help him. I was somewhat confrontational at first when I heard this. Some of these non-profits use federal money to fund their actions, but they aren't actually interested in helping anyone; they just file the paperwork to get the money from the government. And, unfortunately, Deaton's mom was another person who had profited from his addiction, making money from these organizations. Fortunately, it turned out to be legit.

The whole situation put what Jess and I wanted to do front and center. We wanted to help people. I got through the fifty-page application for the non-profit and sent it with a $700 check on April 13, 2021. The mission statement for Flanders Fields was to help homeless veterans. Jess and I were happy and relieved when it was done. In truth, it was our dream come true. But I was also worried it might blow up in my face and trigger the IRS to come after me for some back taxes I owed.

Only time would tell. It was in God's hands now.

Us in Georgia - about 15-20 days clean.

Maddy and James - happy in Georgia

WE FIGHT MONSTERS

Brandon Kelly and James

Brandon Kelly

Ben and Sergeant Brandon Deaton

CHAPTER TEN

THE FALL OF KABUL

JULY 2021

"Hey man, do you want to do something fucking crazy?", asked Jack on the phone.

Around July 2021, USMC intelligence veteran, Jack Britton, connected with me on LinkedIn, asking about my business and experience. I thought he was interested in a business opportunity, but, apparently, he thought I could assist in something else.

My cell was on speaker. It was midnight and I had just picked up my oldest son, Jackson, from his work at a pizza restaurant; he gave me a look as if to say, *here we fucking go again*.

"Of course," I told Jack.

"We're going to get a bunch of people out of Afghanistan. I'll call you tomorrow." Then he hung up.

What the hell?

"What the fuck are you going to do in Afghanistan?", asked my son.

"I have no idea."

I racked my brain thinking of how I could be of any use in Afghanistan. Then, I remembered that he'd been asking me very strange questions in the LinkedIn messages about Black Rifle Co, specifically if the system worked overseas. *I hope this motherfucker doesn't pull me into some illegal shit.*

I immediately called Robert. "Hey man, can we use our Black Rifle Co data gathering system overseas?"

He was matter-of-fact at first. "Well, we are definitely not compliant in Europe. Why do you ask?"

"What about Afghanistan?"

"What the fuck are you talking about, dude?"

"I don't really know. I think someone might be asking me about that soon."

Robert told me he would look into it.

When I got home, I told Jess, and she asked how I could help them.

"I don't know, but I'm going to figure it out because I want to do this."

She was with me 100 percent.

Jack called back the next day, adding me to a bunch of groups on the Signal chat app that included SEALs, Green Berets, and other veterans. "I need you to answer questions these guys have about data," he told me. Jack had gotten a good understanding of what we did with information at Black Rifle Co. "The Taliban has made it to Kunduz. The entire country is about to fall, and the U.S. government won't acknowledge it. People need to move to the capital and onto the last planes out. We need to help them find ground routes, back routes, mountain passes, or fucking anything where there is less phone activity and less probability of a Taliban presence."

Black Rifle Co analyzes cookies to see what kind of content is accessed on devices in the U.S. to focus marketing initiatives, but this was something new. "I'll try to figure it out, Jack. Our data only works in America. However, I know some people who might be able to help."

I spent the next month mapping safe ground routes between Afghan provinces based on the lack of cell phone activity.

My name is Ben Owen. I'm an American volunteer helping evacuate our allies to the Kabul International Airport. Do you need help?

Once I'd done everything I could to help Jack and his friends with safe routes to Kabul, Jack asked for help getting some of the at-risk families to the airport. He had a list of priority names provided by American generals that needed vetting.

That first message was to a guy named Wafa, an interpreter for U.S. forces according to the list. No response. Next up, Pardisi, then Perouz, Rahimi, on and on.

Later, people would ask me why I got involved as deeply as I did. I mean, I didn't know any of these people. I'd never been to Afghanistan, or even to the Middle East. I'd barely been in the military. Yet, how could I say no? It was all over the news. People's lives were at stake. I was living comfortably in Atlanta. My family was healthy. We were well fed. We had jobs and a great house, by the grace of God. It never even occurred to me to turn him down.

I moved to the next name and copied and pasted the same text. No reply.

Getting no traction from the texts, I decided to use an open-source product called Spy Cloud to use the contact information I had and find connected phone numbers and emails. I discovered a U.S. number in Fayetteville, NC, and called it.

"Ashikula Pardisi," came the voice over the phone.

That was a good sign, same last name. I explained who I was and what I was trying to do.

"Yeah, that's my brother. I'm a language teacher here at Fort Bragg." He told me he would reach out to the family and connect me, which he did.

I received proof of life photos of the family, eleven in all, then sent all the information to Jack, who volunteered for the National Child Protection Task Force (NCPTF) and had contacts on the ground that could help. Ultimately, he coordinated for a man called "Santa 6" to pick the family up in a bus, bring them to the airport, and coordinate entry to the airport with U.S. military forces.

Success! I was elated and addicted to helping the next person.

On August 15th, the Taliban took Kabul and the evacuation shifted into high gear. Everyone in the Afghan Signal groups shared their success stories and helped each other out. There were a lot of warnings about possible vehicle bombs near the Abbey Gate, but nothing specific. One member asked if I could help get his interpreter to the Airport, a man named Monir who had a pregnant wife and five kids.

I called Jack to see if we could use his resources to help.

"Have you confirmed they served U.S. forces?", he asked.

"Yeah, a 10th Mountain veteran in the Signal room vouched that he served with his unit. He also has texts of the Taliban threatening to kill him and rape his pregnant wife."

"Okay, I'm going to give you contact info for Santa 6 and the U.S. Marine HQ at the airport so you can coordinate getting him inside."

Monir was receiving conflicting information from another American named Josh who was trying to convince him to go to Abbey Gate, but I could see on the Signal channel that a lot of people were having trouble getting in there, and I had just had some success at Black Gate.

Fuck that guy Josh, I texted. *Head for Black Gate. I have a guy waiting to get you inside there. Have your red scarf showing so he can recognize you.*

I texted Santa 6 to tell him Monir was heading to the gate.

My phone rang.

"I can't get to Black Gate. The Talibs are blocking the way," said Monir. "They just shot up my car."

Fuck! Now what?

"Fuck these guys, bro!", I heard Monir yell. Then I heard a car engine rev, followed by a sound like that of a car hitting a speed bump too fast. Boomp-boomp. Then more yelling.

My other phone rang. Santa 6.

"Where's your guy? I have another pickup."

Then, Monir yelled into the phone. "I made it. I see the gate. There's a bunch of cars blocking the way."

My heart was racing. "What happened?"

"I just drove straight at them and they didn't move out of the way, so I ran those fuckers down." I heard a car door slam shut. "I'm ditching the car."

"Wave your scarf. They're looking for you!"

"I see the scarf," said Santa 6. "I see him."

Monir kept me on the line as he maneuvered toward the gate and Santa 6. I heard them greet each other.

"We're in," said Monir. Then he paused, and I heard him yelling to someone else. "Hey bro." I heard the jingle of keys. "Keep the car. I won't need it where I'm going."

Two down.

"They're not going to let Mohammed in, just so you know," I told Irfanullah. "So, go ahead and have that hard conversation with him."

Irfanullah was the leader of the eight-member family I'd sent Santa 6 to bring in. They had already tried to get into Abbey Gate twice with no luck, and Santa 6 was bringing them to Black Gate. While vetting all of their documents, I realized Mohammed was an Afghan married to a Lawful Permanent Resident with a U.S. green card, but they had only gotten married two weeks earlier, and their marriage certificate was only in Dari. It was very unlikely the American soldiers would allow him in.

"I'm not going to tell him. The Americans are going to do the right thing and let him in," Irfanullah told me.

Got to love his naivety.

By that time, I'd been working with families for about a week. A few made it through the gates, but just as many didn't, and each one felt personal. For better or worse, I was connected to these people from the second I spoke to them and became their shepherd to freedom.

At the gate, Santa 6 convinced the Americans to let seven family members in, but Mohammed was forced to tell his bride goodbye at the gate and watch her leave, not knowing if he would ever see her again.

It was heartbreaking.

For almost ten days straight, I stayed up pretty much twenty-four hours a day, sitting in the basement and using every tool I could think of to call and vet people and coordinate movement to the airport. Jessica was super supportive, even though she didn't understand everything that was going on. She brought me food and fresh clothes every now and again, even insisting I bathe once in a while. I basically only left for bathroom breaks. I must have spoken with over one hundred families in total. My oldest kids and my parents probably thought I had relapsed.

On August 26th, I made another attempt with a family that had already tried unsuccessfully once. This time, I'd made contact with the Marines inside. I guided them just outside of the Abbey gate. My phone dinged, and I stared at the photo I'd received.

This had to work. No Marine could ignore those signs.

Eight family members held twenty-inch square signs in thick black writing that read:
CHESTY PULLER
TEUFEL HUNDEN
10 NOV 1775

Chesty Puller was the most famous Marine in history, someone all Marines knew. Teufel Hunden was German for Hell Hound or Devil Dog, a nickname the Germans had for the American Marines in WWI, and the date was the day the Marines were founded.

This time, the Marines were looking for them, and a squad waded out into the crowd.

I received another photo from the family showing they had linked up with the Marines and were being escorted back to Abbey Gate, then I turned my attention to another family I'd been simultaneously helping.

The Perouz family consisted of three brothers with their wives and children, a total of thirteen people. I guided them closer to Abbey Gate. Just a couple more minutes and they'd be within sight.

Then Wafa Anoosh, the first family I'd tried to contact on August 15th, finally returned my text. Thirteen family members. I needed to coordinate a bus to Black Gate.

Can we fit a wheelchair in the bus? Wafa texted me.

What the hell? From the photos he'd sent me, there were no elderly people.

My two-year-old daughter has Cerebral Palsy.

Crap. This wasn't going to work. I'd already had a few families almost get trampled to death, and, eventually, the family would need to push their way through crowds.

Stand by, I texted. *I need to think of a new plan.*

I turned my attention back to the Perouz family, who were close to Abbey Gate. I had recruited Jessica to help me talk with the women and calm them down while I spoke to the eldest brother, Yasin. When I kept losing my connection with them, I suspected someone was using a jammer, but I didn't know if it was the good guys or the bad guys.

Finally, we had a solid connection, and I saw Yasin on video. "Listen up, go toward the gate. The Americans are looking for your red—" Suddenly, there was a loud explosion, and the phone spun through the air. Smoke and dirt were everywhere.

What the hell?

I yelled, then threw my chair across the room.

Jessica ran into the room. "What happened?"

"A fucking bomb went off!"

Shit! Shit! Shit! I'd been receiving warnings all morning that this might happen.

Had the Chesty Puller family made it in?

Had I led the Perouz family to their death?

Someone picked up the phone, and I saw Yasin again. Thank God.

"Are you all right?" I asked.

"Yes. We're all alright." He panned around. There was blood and destruction everywhere. I heard gunfire, women screaming, and children crying as they held body parts of what used to be their parents. "RUN," I yelled into the phone. "Get your family out of there, NOW. Abbey Gate is over with!"

The line went dead.

Kabul Afghanistan 8/15/2021

The Pardisi Family, first successful evacuation

Momand Family

WE FIGHT MONSTERS

Monir Family

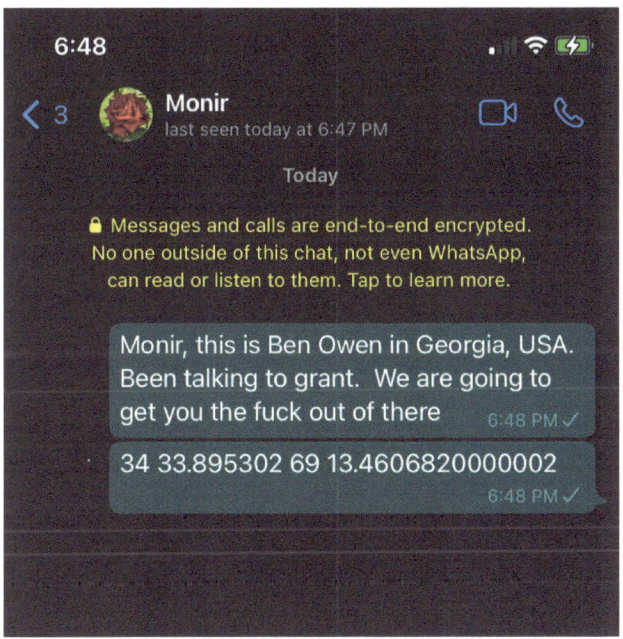

First contact with Monir, sending him coordinates to where I needed him to move to.

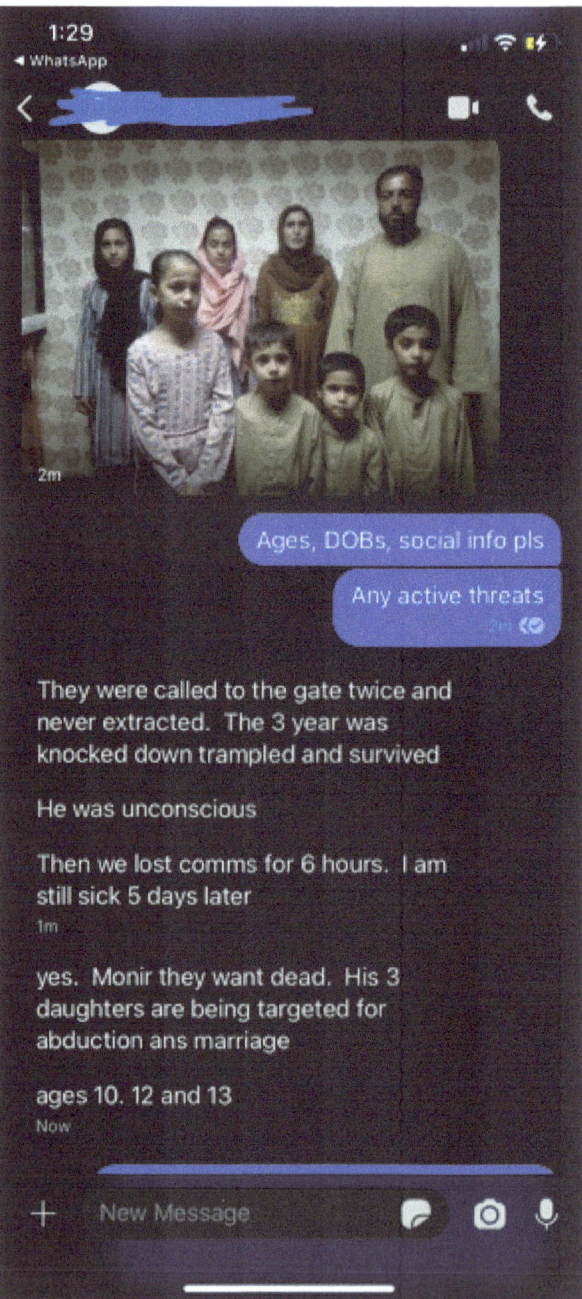

Getting tapped in to assist with Monir.

Monir arrived to black gate, proof of life sent and working getting Santa 6 to his location.

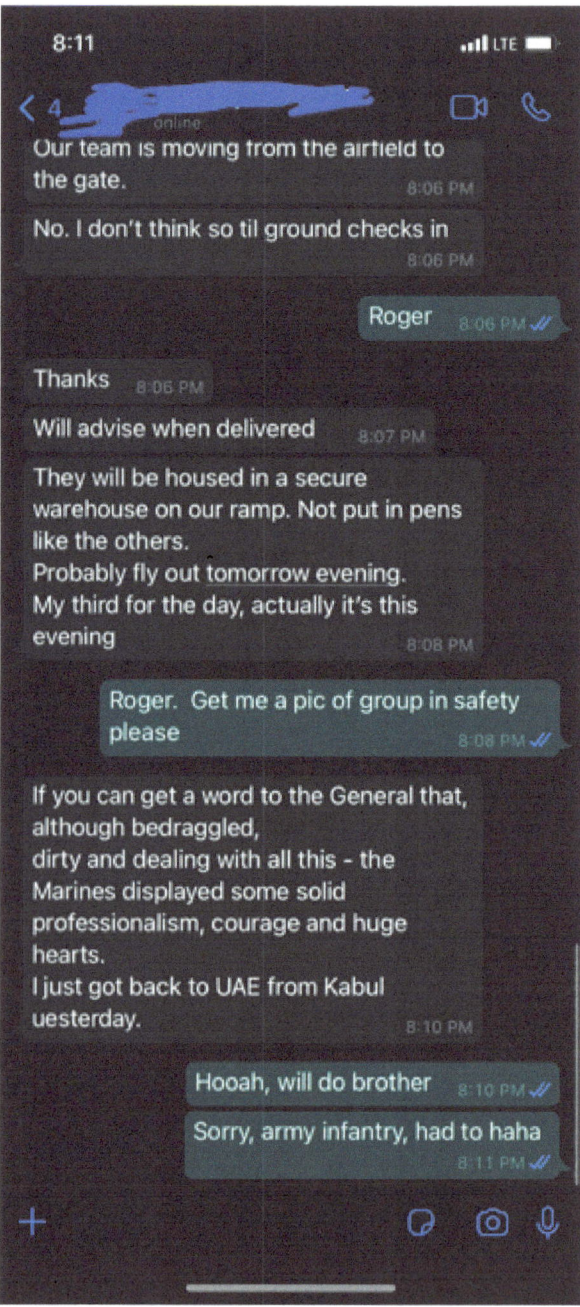

Working with SOF outside HKIA to move families in via Abbey and Black Gates.

WE FIGHT MONSTERS

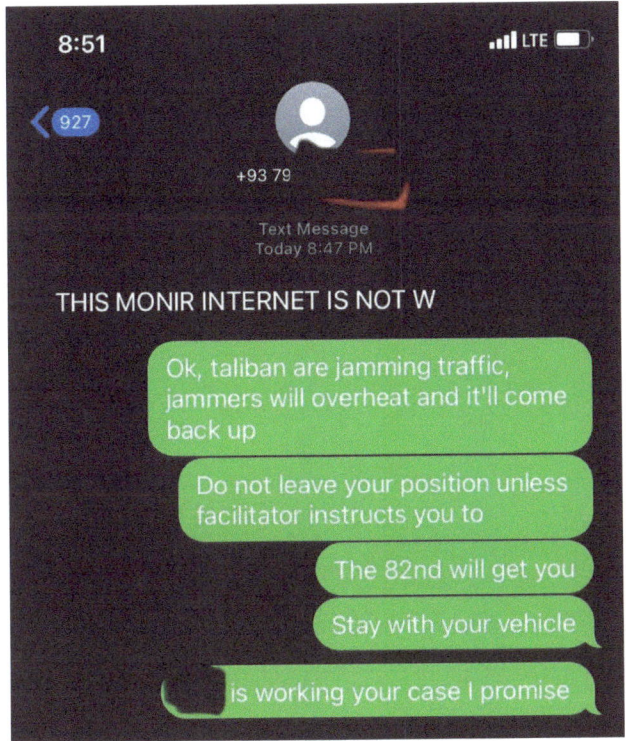

Things getting spicy

Monir's bullet riddled car that he "donated" to the 82nd.

High view of real time maps being used to navigate ground routes.

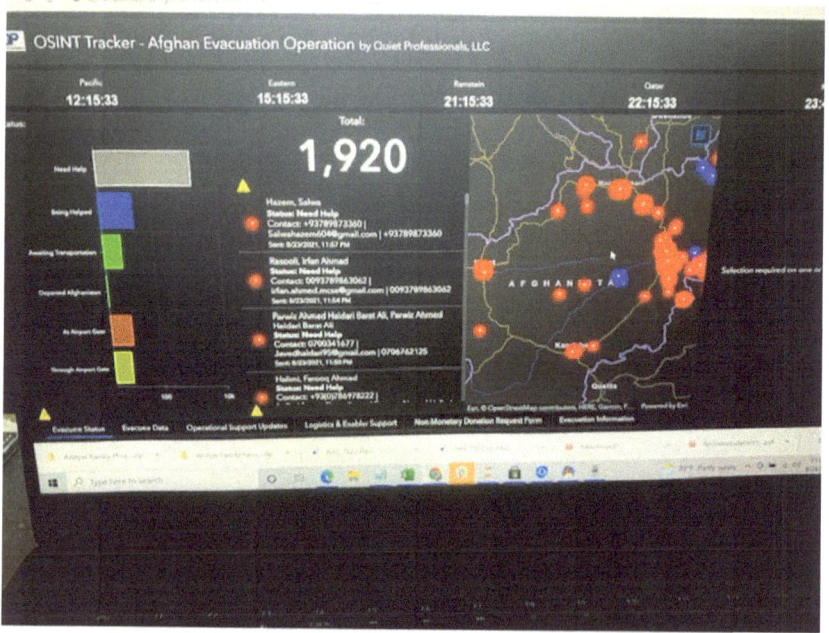

Active case load of gunshots, bomb threats, VBIEDs, medevacswefc.

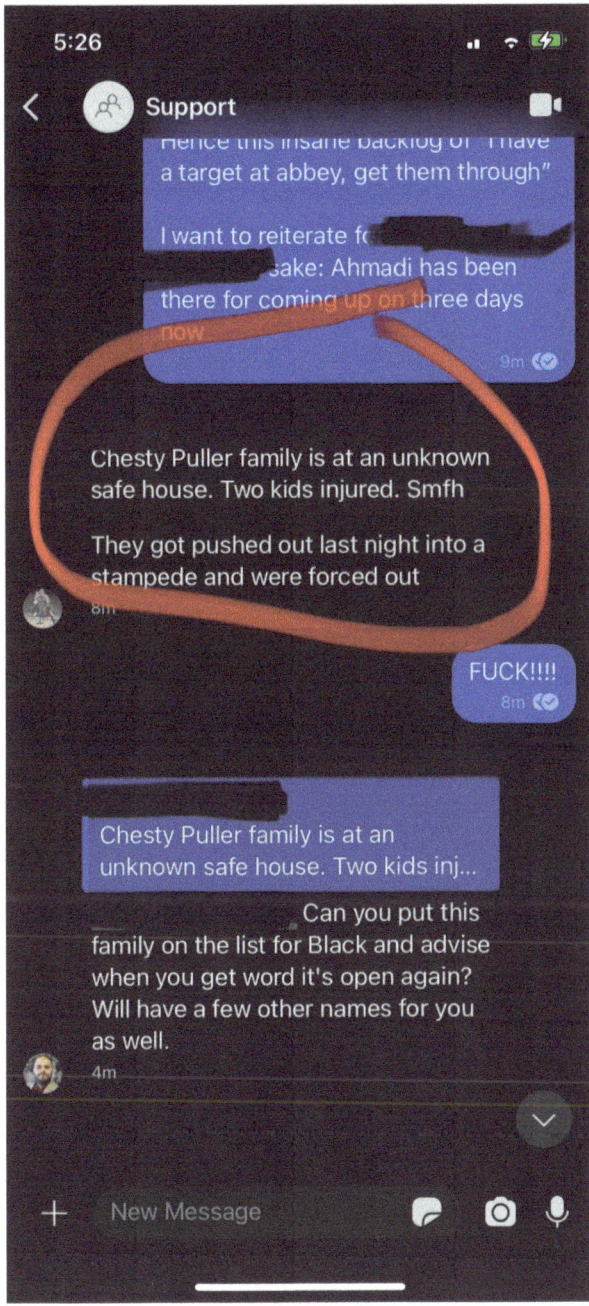

Chesty Puller family texts

Chesty Puller Family

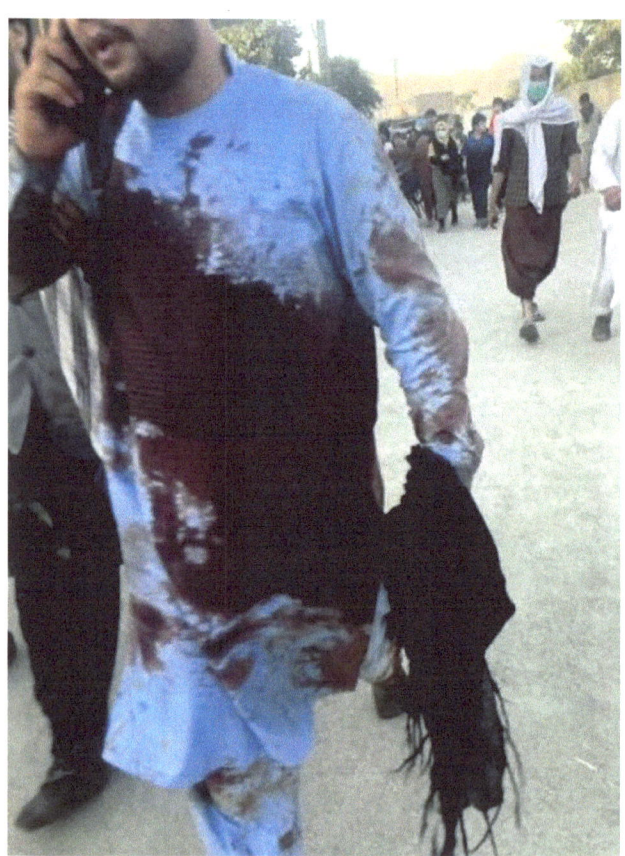

After Abby Gate bombing

CHAPTER ELEVEN

THERE WAS STILL HOPE

AUGUST 2021

THERE WAS STILL HOPE.

I could feel the mission atmosphere change after the explosion. When the bomb went off, it killed thirteen U.S. soldiers and an unknown number of Afghans. There was chatter that the U.S. security forces would still let people into the airport if they had a blue passport, but no one else, at least for the moment. That was the hope.

The Chesty Puller family had made it through Abbey Gate just before the bomb exploded, but the Perouz and the Wafa families were on standby until further notice.

I called Pardisi, the brother of the first family I had rescued, who was a U.S. resident and working as a language instructor. "Hey man, I need to rent safe houses in Kabul for the families that didn't make it out. Can you help?"

"Yeah, man, I got a cousin in Kabul." He gave me a phone number just as I received a text about an American citizen named Nasria who had a blue passport and was stuck in Kabul. I asked Jessica to start working on the safe houses while I tried to help this woman.

Someone had seen Nasria get smacked around by the Taliban

outside Abbey Gate while her boyfriend got beat up. They found her number on a Facebook Live she made after the event which showed her on the street talking about how the Taliban had beat her even though she was obviously a pregnant American, and the U.S. government didn't give a shit.

I texted her. *My name is Ben Owen. Do you need help getting to the airport?*

The Marines and the Army don't give a fuck! Nasria texted back. *Those Taliban mother fuckers have our vehicles and weapons, and they're using them against us.*

I can get you out. You have a blue passport. I can help.

They wouldn't give me the time of day at Abbey Gate. I'm not leaving without my boyfriend. I don't give a fuck. I'm not leaving without him. Let them kill me. You can't fuck up anyone if they're already dead.

If she didn't want my help, I couldn't dedicate more time to her because there were still families who were stuck and feared for their lives, and I was linked to them now. I had been part of the system that had convinced them to leave all of their belongings and go to Kabul with their families. Now they were targets, and I felt like their lives were in my hands because no one else was coming to help them.

I continued to text Nasria as I helped Jessica with the safe houses, trying to convince her to come back and try again without her boyfriend. Finally, on August 31, one of the U.S. SOF guys inside the airport told me in a chat room that he could go outside and grab her.

Send me a photo of your passport now. I have someone who can bring you in, I texted her.

Dude, stop giving my number away. It's not cool. Random people are messaging me asking me for my passport.

They're trying to get you out.

She refused to come to the airport. Her comments were peppered with so many swear words, Jessica and I began referring to her as Afghan Jessica.

That evening, the last American plane left Afghanistan, and the Taliban filled the sky with bullets in celebration; many of the people I had tried to help sent me photos, and it looked like some kind of messed up 4th of July.

Nasria started another Facebook Live outside of her apartment. "Motherfucking America is a bunch of bitches and cowards. Look at all the equipment they left behind in the hands of the Taliban." She then panned around the street, showing the Taliban shooting at the sky and all the equipment in their possession.

I tried to reach her Congressman in California, but Nasria stopped talking to me. The unfortunate reality was that some Afghans chose not to face the dangers of trying to make it through the gates. Others did and still didn't make it through, instead bringing harm to their families. Only a lucky few made it onto the planes leaving the country. There wasn't anything else I could do for her at that moment if she was going to ghost me, and I had a lot of other things on my plate.

Also, the Chesty Puller story went viral within twenty-four hours of the family getting in, mentioning my name in the story, so my phone was blowing up with requests for help. Most of them didn't have blue passports, which meant there was nothing I could do but find them a place to wait out the storm.

August 31, 2021

Within twenty-four hours, Jessica and I became Kabul slum lords.

Pardisi's cousin managed to find three houses, and we sent him $1,000 through MoneyGram. Then, we linked him to the Wafa and Perouz families so we could get them off the street. Our phones were ringing off the hook due to the Chesty Puller exposure. By the end of the week, we had twenty families housed in ten houses.

The Afghans we had under our protection didn't know Kabul and were wanted by the Taliban, especially the women who had been police officers, so it wasn't safe for them to leave the houses. Ever since Mohammed had been forced to leave his American wife at Black Gate during the evacuation, he'd continued to communicate with us, asking if there was anything we could do to help him get out. There wasn't, but Jess texted him to see if he would help us. *Would you be interested in being one of our drivers? You'd deliver supplies to the people who can't leave their houses.*

He'd been following Flanders Fields on social media and immediately replied, *I will be happy to do that. I will do my best for you.*

We sent him money and a list: blankets, food, firewood, and other necessities. Honestly, we were making this up as we went along; we had literally been crackheads on the streets of Memphis only two years earlier. Jess gave Mohammad the first family's phone number so they could communicate and told the family to expect his call. Then we told Mohammad to take a photo of the family receiving the supplies once they were delivered.

A few minutes later, we received the photo. *Holy crap*, I thought. *This shit works. We can do this.*

September 7, 2021

Kabul was getting dangerous.

I dove back into my tech, mapping patterns of life and device activity between Kabul and Mazar-i-Sharif. Some of the non-profit organizations I spoke to in the chat rooms were claiming that the airport in Mazar was the only option to continue flying out endangered Afghans. With the help of our real estate contact, I got a hold of a bus driver to move the Wafa family and forked out $4,500. We didn't know better. We learned fast, though. $450 was what it probably should have cost.

Our real estate agent in Kabul had a cousin in Mazar, and we expanded our slumlord empire to include that city, eventually renting over fifty properties over the next month between the two cities. When I think about it now, it was surreal. Jessica and I had never even been to Afghanistan, and we were probably managing more properties there than any actual citizen. By the end of September, we had become more familiar with the inner workings and just how to get shit done in the country than a pair of addicts had any business doing. Jess and I were consistently running on barely any sleep, something we had plenty of experience with due to our addictions, though it was significantly harder without the crack fuel.

Because of my tech capabilities, Jack asked me to jump into this evacuation, and I'd agreed on a whim. After starting as relatively unknown to the other people in the chat rooms, within two months, we became the go-to group to get things done. And it wasn't that we were smarter or had more money than the others, but we'd been homeless, so we knew how to make deals. Trading weapons caches for a month's rent, exchanging food for medical supplies. Some would call it God, others the universe, but in a way, it seemed like we had been training our whole lives to be exactly where we were: making a difference for people on the other side of the world, saving lives.

Until now, we'd spent a lot of our own money, even digging into our kids' college funds. About this time, Robert brought up a good point that we hadn't considered.

"They're vets."

"What?" I didn't understand what he was getting at. Vets? Who was a vet?

He held up a letter. "Jessica showed this to me last week. We received our 501c3 approval for Flanders Fields in the mail while you were working in the basement. Our charter is to house homeless vets." He paused, allowing me to put two and two together. "Nothing says they have to be American vets."

He was right, of course. I immediately turned my gifts to raising money on LinkedIn for Flanders to help the countryless Afghan SOF vets.

Other organizations had rented hotel rooms for the Afghans they supported in Mazar, but they quickly ran out of money. We were the first organization that had leased houses (mainly because we didn't have the money to put everyone in hotels), so we opened up our properties to support who we could, including people that the Taliban were actively hunting. We received housing requests from other non-profits such as Task Force Argo and Operation North Star who were trying to help the same demographic of Afghans. It made sense to share resources, as we were all trying to accomplish the same objective. Only a few planes landed to take out VIPs to Abu Dhabi, and, fortunately, a dozen or so of our Afghans were offered seats on the flights out.

On top of the concern for safe housing in Afghanistan, we had to find countries that would allow refugees so they could wait out the visa process. I connected with a man named Josh Jenkins in the chat rooms who was going to Kosovo to coordinate their capability to receive Afghans. It took a while, but we eventually figured out he was the same Josh I'd been in a pissing match with, trying to get Monir to Abbey Gate when I wanted him to go meet Santa 6 at Black Gate. We may not have started off on the best footing with one another, but it all worked out. His ability to get good things done in bad places was rapidly made apparent. We decided to hit our evacuation problem from both sides. So, while he was in Kosovo, Robert and I went to DC to speak to the Kosovar Ambassador at their embassy. Josh coordinated a humanitarian city using privately donated and funded land. For some reason, the U.S. State Department was working against us. The Kosovar Ambassador had been informed by the State Department that any flights into his country outside of sanctioned U.S. military operations would be considered human smuggling and the Kosovar government should stand down from helping non-profits.

I returned to Atlanta with a different view of the government, seriously embracing the old tongue-in-cheek saying, "I'm with the government. I'm here to help." Not. Definitely not.

September 14, 2021

I was going to Tajikistan.

During my trip to DC, Jessica informed me that some of our houses were being raided. We were hiding some high-value Afghan judges, and the Taliban were actively hunting them. No more planes were coming, so I started looking for alternative methods.

I had received information from a Black Rifle Co client about a place on the Panj River, near the Panji Poyon Friendship Bridge, that could be crossed easily from Afghanistan. Josh returned from Kosovo, and then found out about the route through Tajikistan. He told me that he could contact a friend of his in the Tajik government and provide helicopters for an evacuation from Mazar-i-Sharif. Unfortunately, the State Department had passed the same warning to the Tajik government as the Kosovar government—no aiding non-U.S. government entities to move personnel from Afghanistan or they will be accused of human trafficking. So, I proceeded with my plan to cross the Panj River. I sent some Afghan SOF guys there to do a recon. They confirmed the information, but said it would require some swimming and wading. Almost all the people we were trying to help had small children, many of whom were disabled. We needed a boat.

Fuck it.

"Jessica, this Tajikistan plan looks possible, but it's complicated, and as much as we love our Afghan SOF guys, we need somebody on the ground on the Tajik side. I want to go." I thought she'd say hell no.

"Fuck yeah, do it." That's why I love her. I should have known better. She was as fully invested as I was.

I bought plane tickets to the capital, Dushanbe, and rented a room. Someone told me I should coordinate with the embassy, but when I called, they were useless. Then I decided I needed to figure out how to back channel the operation. I used my tech gift to identify specific people at the embassy who might help and found a personal number for a chief consular who I called.

"Have you ever been to Tajikistan?" he asked after I told him what I planned on doing.

"I've never even been out of the U.S."

"How the fuck are you going to get around? Are you out of your mind?"

It wasn't going the way I wanted; that's for sure. "Look, I'm involved in the Afghan evacuation."

"I cannot encourage you in strong enough terms to not cross the Panj River if that's what you're thinking about doing." He paused. "That being said, you need to know your way around the city and the country before you get here or get a guide."

We ended the call. I was a little stumped. I started googling Tajikistan, wondering if I might be able to familiarize myself with its geography like I did with Kabul, but there was no way. Due to the twenty-year war, there was just a boatload of detailed information about Afghanistan; not so with Tajikistan. I found my hostel room on Caravanistan, a website for hikers, and it looked promising as I skimmed through the comments. And that's where I found Nikki.

She had just come back from hiking in Afghanistan and Tajikistan the month prior during the Taliban invasion. There were a lot of crazy people on the website, but crazy was what I needed. On her website, she advertised that she led tours, and she lived in Alaska. I shot her a message, hoping against hope that she was my girl.

Hey, my name is Ben, and I'm doing this weird shit, trying to evacuate people from Afghanistan. I'd love to pick your brain on ground routes between Afghanistan and Tajikistan.

Two minutes later, I got a response. *Are you evacuating Afghans?*
Yes, I am.
And you want my help?
Yes, I do.
When?
Fuck yes! I thought. *I'll be there on September 24th,* I told her.
I'm in, and you don't even have to buy me a ticket, she continued. *Meet me in Dushanbe.*

Then, I realized I didn't have a passport. I'd never had a passport. Word got around in the chat rooms that I needed one, and suddenly I had congressional chiefs of staff and military legislative assistants calling my phone. I had no idea they knew I even existed. Unknown to me, I'd been housing their Afghans of interest when the planes stopped coming to Mazar; I didn't know who they were or worked for because everyone was using different handles in the chat rooms. Out of the blue, I got an emergency passport appointment in New Orleans in two days.

When I showed up for my appointment, they handed me a piece of paper stating that the Department of Treasury was denying my request for a passport because I had a delinquent tax debt from 2012. While I'd accomplished a lot in the last few years of sobriety, Erin and I had made some big errors in our taxes nearly eight years ago when we were running ReTech that resulted in us erroneously owing more than two hundred thousand dollars to the government. And just like that, the operation shut down.

A couple of days later, the judges were killed by the Taliban.

October 5, 2021

"Cut the shit," said the female MP. "What the fuck do you have going on?"

"What are you talking about?", I countered. But I knew exactly what she was talking about. I had been afraid of this when I'd been asked to speak to the U. S. Army Special Operations Command (USASOC) at Fort Bragg, NC. I was barely a veteran. In reality, I was a former addict with a rap sheet a mile long. What the hell was I doing there?

"Stop," she told me. "Level with me."

"Okay, yeah. I got a little bit of a background, but it's no big deal."

"Bro, you've got fourteen convictions for guns and drugs. Believe me, it's a big deal."

"Wait a minute, I wasn't convicted, everything was reduced to a misdemeanor." I then proceeded to tell her about my background with the law and why I was here. "Only misdemeanors, but no felony convictions," I finished.

"Okay, but your criminal background check came back with fourteen felonies, which makes you a felon unless you can prove you're not. Is there anyone that can corroborate your story?"

I thought for a second. "Actually, yes there is." I called Bryan Owens from the Shelby County Drug Court in Memphis and explained what was going on.

"How can I help?" he asked. He knew Jess and I were clean and followed us on social media.

"The MP needs to hear from Judge Dwyer."

"Well, I just happen to be in court with the judge right now. Put her on the phone."

I handed the phone to the MP, and she said, "I've got a Benjamin Owen here."

They talked back and forth, and then she gave the phone back. "Wait here." She returned a few minutes later and said, "You're cool. Also, the judge vouched for you, too. We're good."

She printed me out a base pass with my last active duty photo from Fort Benning, GA twenty years prior, and I laughed my ass off.

We then headed over to the USASOC building.

I'd been called a week earlier while I was still trying to figure out the Tajikistan operation. Some guys in one of the chat rooms needed help getting some of the interpreter's families out of Afghanistan, and they were enamored by my ability to find safe routes.

I was escorted into a big classroom with a large whiteboard, and someone handed me a marker. There were about twenty Afghan interpreters there, most of them sobbing, talking about their families who had been left behind and were in danger.

Suddenly, a sergeant major walked in. "Shut the hell up!", he told everyone. "Help has arrived. Ben's going to get them out."

I was shocked. "Hold the fuck up for a minute, Sergeant Major. I think I need to set expectations here."

I explained my methodology for vetting Afghans and determining safe routes. By then, Jessica and I had a bunch of safe houses in Kabul, and I agreed to help house some of the families who didn't have anywhere to go. They also spoke about some future flights they had planned to evacuate people from Mazar-i-Sharif. Maybe I could get some of my people out on those as well.

The whole time, I just couldn't believe that I was the guy they were coming to for help. I figured the government would have better assets than a drug addict.

October 6, 2021

Mohammad was still bringing aid to our houses in Kabul. We would usually pad the money we sent to him with an additional $100 dollars so he could survive. One time he asked us, "What do you want me to do with all the extra money you've sent?"

"That's for you," I told him.

"I don't need it. I'll buy extra supplies for the people we are helping."

He never took a dime from us.

We learned a lot about interpersonal relationships in our Afghan dealings. Some families would call the Taliban authorities on other families because of a disagreement or slight. We had an apartment full of single male commandos who were getting antsy and bored, so we hired them to do what Mohammad was doing for us in Kabul and also address any dangerous situations if they came up.

Sometimes the Taliban would conduct a surprise raid on one of our safe houses or capture someone we were trying to help. One of the first things they would do was search any cell phones for U.S. numbers and send videos to those numbers. If they were trying to discourage us, it failed miserably, because it just made us mad and more determined than ever to help.

One female police officer was taken. The Taliban raped her, then sent me the video. The Wafa family's house was raided, but the men hid and the women shamed the Taliban so much that they left them alone. We quickly moved them with the help of our Afghan SOF fixers. I got another video from the Taliban showing them running over a father and shooting a mother; I don't know what happened to the kids. Once, the Taliban surrounded a building where an Afghan SOF guy named Ghulam was hiding. We'd sent him to do a recon for a land route to evacuate other Afghans. He had been granted a visa to the U.S. but was unable to make it to the airport before the last plane left, and now he knew he was about to be captured and probably killed. He sent us a video right before they broke down the door, "I'm sorry I've let you down, brothers. This is not your fault. You guys have done all you can. This isn't even your government's fault." We never heard from him again.

Unfortunately, Flanders wasn't making nearly enough money to cover all our expenses, but we couldn't in good conscience stop. Every time we thought about what these people must be going through and compared it to how we were living, there was no choice. Before long, we'd spent over seventeen thousand dollars of our own money supporting over six hundred Afghans in sixty-eight houses across Afghanistan.

By the time December rolled around, we were running out of money.

It was getting almost impossible to help people in Afghanistan and run two businesses. Robert took over most of the heavy lifting by running Black Rifle Co, freeing up more time for Jess and me. We decided to sell ReTech, which allowed us to expand Flanders Fields for what we had originally intended it to do. Help vets with addiction.

Two days before Christmas, as we were shutting down safe houses and helping the residents find odd jobs to support themselves, I walked into the living room to find Jess a sobbing mess.

"I know we're broke, and whittling down the safe house operation, but there's something different about this girl, Ben, we have to do something."

I know the look she was giving me well; she wasn't backing down from this one. I sat down on the couch next to her, put my arm around her, and asked her to bring me up to speed. She went to WhatsApp and pressed play on a voice note that had been sent to her. The room was filled with the sound of a woman sobbing. Deep, guttural pain escaped the speaker of the phone.

"The girl who contacted me, her name is Arezo, and this is her mother in the voice note. This was them having to watch as the Taliban were beating the shit out of Arezo's dad." Jess started crying again.

"This isn't fucking fair, Ben! Her dad helped our troops, and this is how we repay them, by leaving them all to be slaughtered?!" Her anger became more palpable the longer she spoke.

She wasn't angry at me. She was hurt and frustrated knowing this is how our government said thank you to our allies. We were all living our cushioned lives in America, while families were being torn apart at the hands of the Taliban.

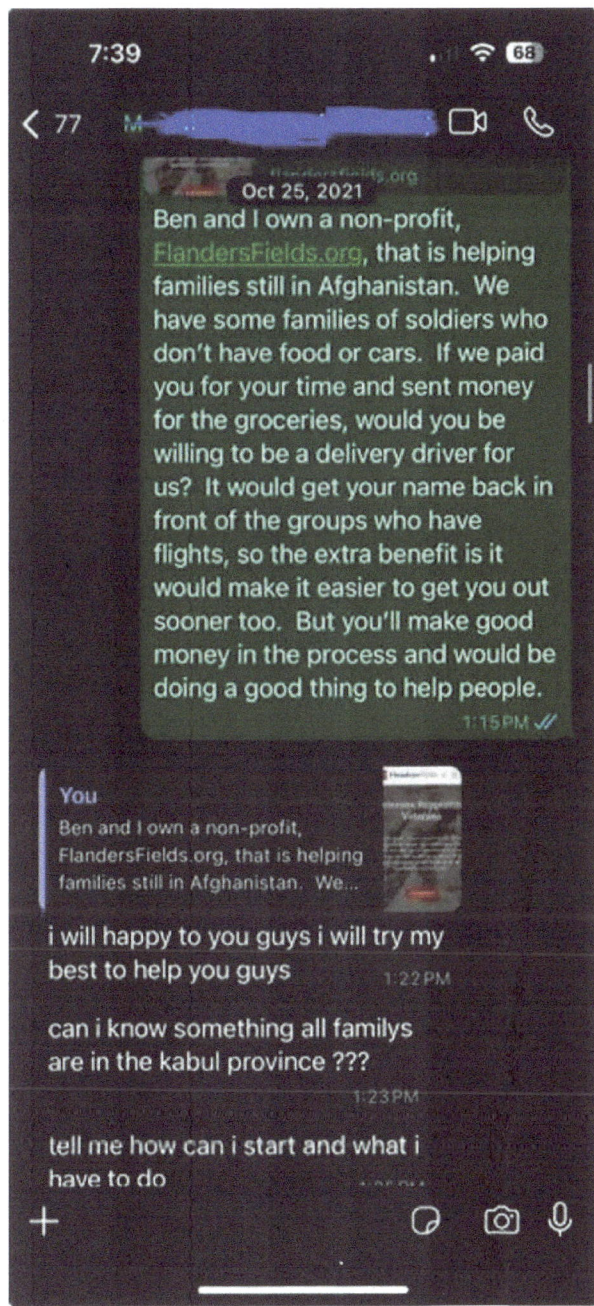

Jess asking Mohammad to be our driver.

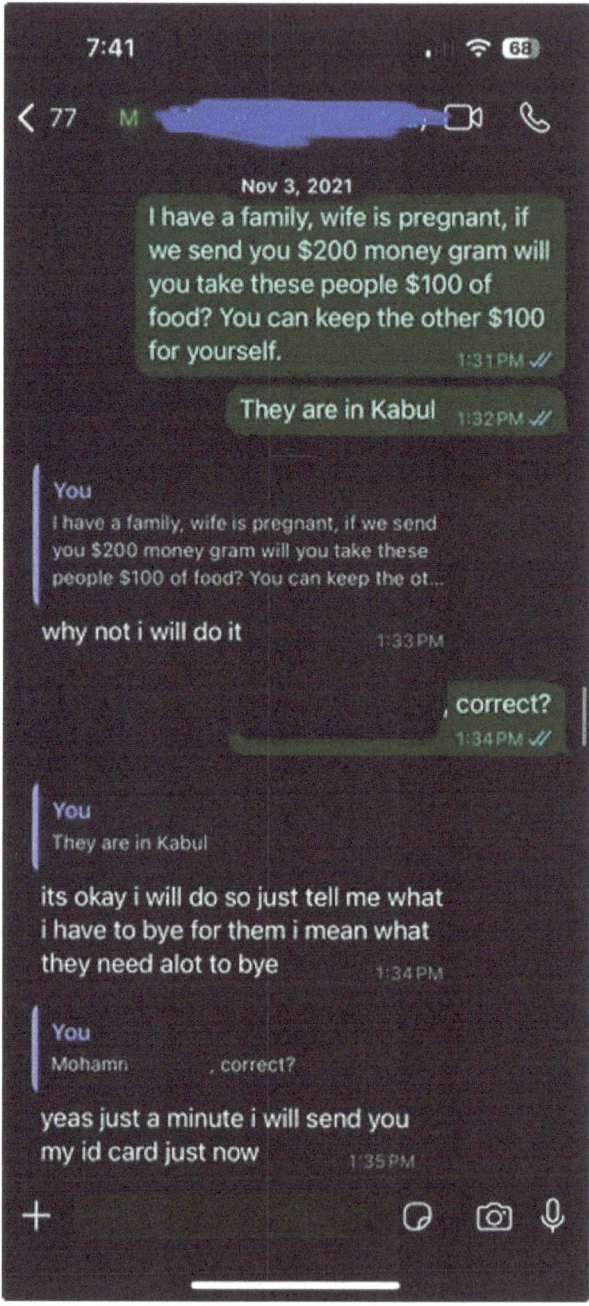

Mohammad getting instructions to help one of the families.

Matt Trompeter, Ben Owen, Robert Colemen, and Berat Gegaj at the Kosovo Embassy.

The picture that was printed out at USASOC (Ben's last picture as active duty)

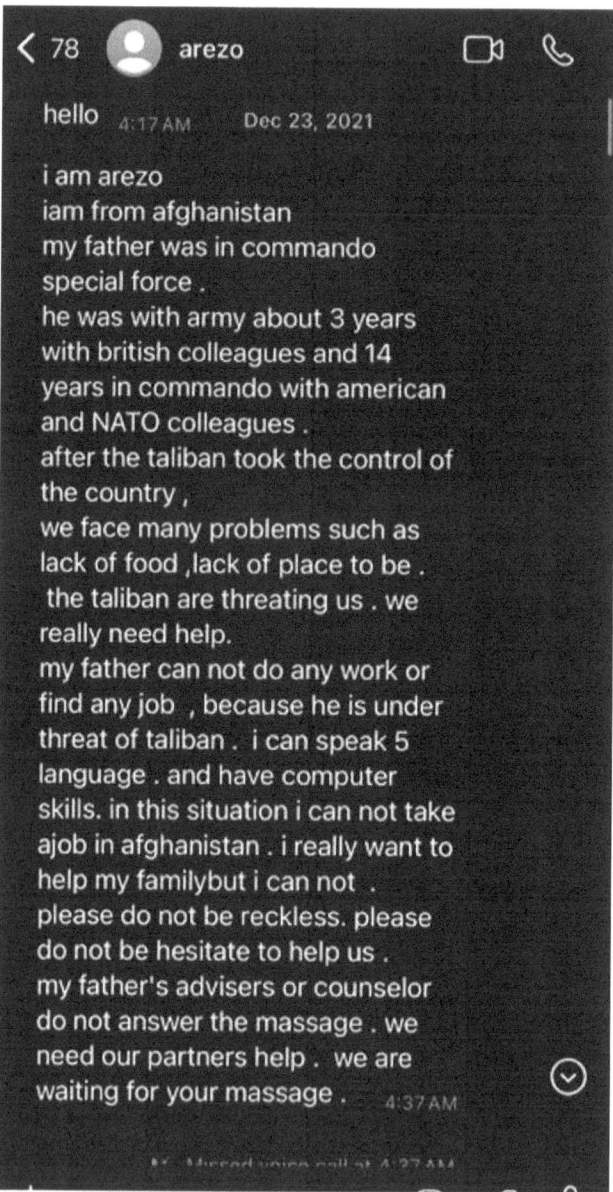

Arezo makes contact with Jess.

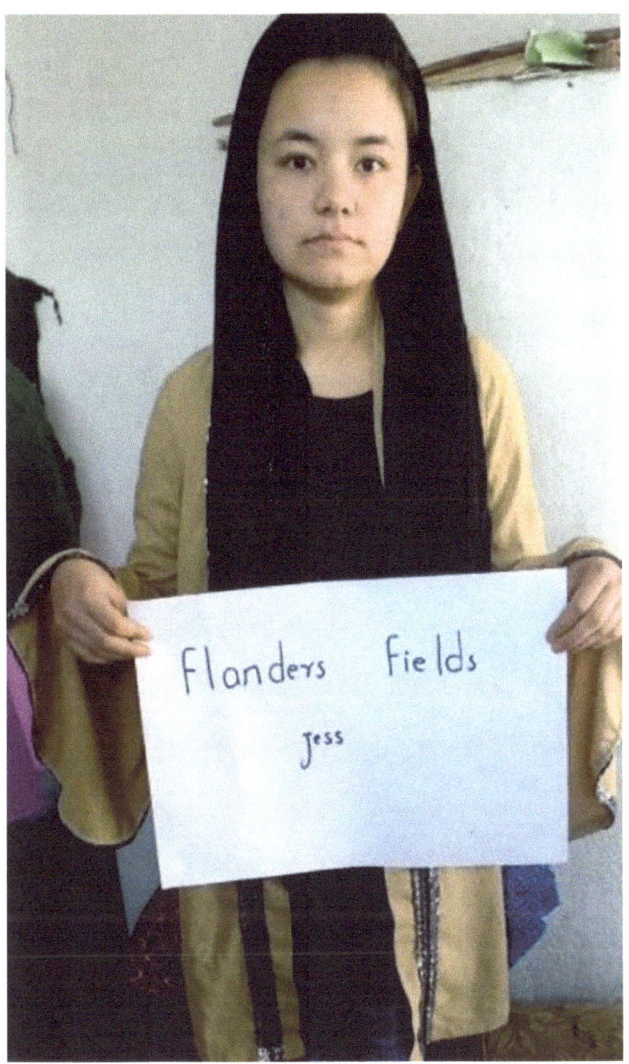

Arezo's proof of life picture.

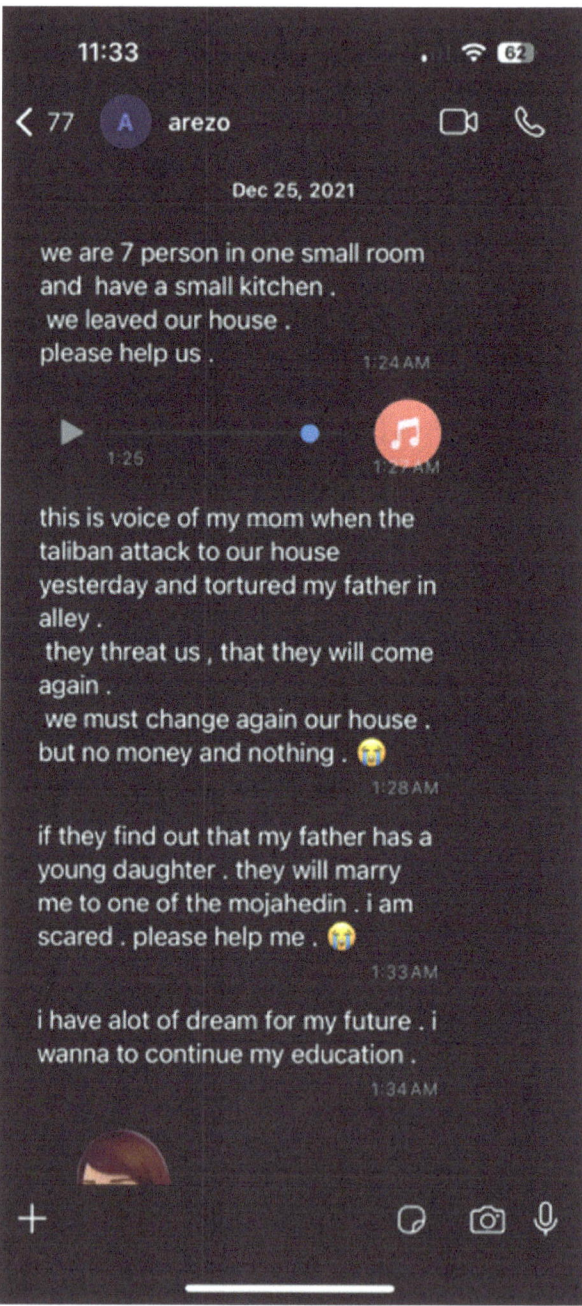

The voice note that changed everything.

CHAPTER TWELVE

TRANSITIONS

FEB 2022

"Okay, Ben, so what's this about?", asked Judge Dwyer.

Jessica, Robert, and I had come to get a letter of recommendation from the drug court judge in Memphis for my next Flanders project. I wasn't sure how this was going to go. While I'd continued sending money to the drug court for them to help other addicts, I didn't have any idea if that had changed the judge's opinion of me.

Tony Shelby was also present, the owner of Rebos halfway house where I was kicked out after 8 days and then spent a lot of time as a recovering addict. Obviously, the drug court judge and the owner of the local halfway house had been working together, and any conversation that involved housing addicts and sober living, even if it was outside of their city limits, should involve Tony. Also, when we did start working in Chattanooga, we were hoping that Tony would mentor us since he already had so much experience.

"Well Judge, I'm buying properties in Chattanooga to make halfway houses for homeless vets using my non-profit, Flanders Fields."

He nodded. "That's a great idea, and I'm sure they need it over there. I'll give you the letter. But why don't y'all do that here in Memphis?"

"I didn't want to step on Tony's toes." I nodded to Tony, who sat in the corner.

"Why don't you just buy Rebos?", the judge asked.

I paused in surprise. "Well, I didn't know it was for sale."

"It is now," Tony piped up.

This was crazy. I had the opportunity to own and operate the same halfway house I'd been kicked out of? I was stunned. Then I came back to reality.

"There's no way I can raise the money for that place. What's it cost?"

"Six hundred grand."

I laughed at the number. It really didn't matter how much the property was selling for. We barely had enough to support the Afghans and our other current operations. "I'm sure I speak for Jessica when I say we'd love to run it. It would mean the world to us. But like I said, Flanders doesn't have that kind of money."

"Let's talk," said Tony. "I'm not retiring until October. If you can raise the money by then, we're good. I won't offer it to anyone else until then. You and Jess are the right people to run it."

Leaving the courthouse that day, our heads were in the clouds. Never in our wildest dreams would we have imagined this before. It wouldn't be easy. After all, we were still using most of Flanders' money for the Afghans. Still, I was leaving with the recommendation from the Judge, and the possibility that someday I'd make owning Rebos a reality.

February, 2022

After we moved Wafa and his family—the Taliban had visited them at one of our safe houses in Mazar—I'd taken a deep dive into their documentation, trying to find additional information that I could use to justify a Special Immigration Visa (SIV). I started running into phone numbers of Americans that might be able to verify the work he'd done for the U.S. government. To tell the truth, I wasn't hopeful, but I didn't stop trying.

"Hi, my name's Ben Owen, and I'm looking for someone named Braden who served with 10th Mountain in Afghanistan."

"Speaking."

I'd found a tenuous connection to Braden as I was running down all possible threads in his paperwork and explained that I was working to get Wafa and his family issued SIVs so they could leave Afghanistan and come to the U.S.

"You fuckers aren't doing enough for those people. They deserve better than being left behind."

I was a little surprised by his anger. "Look, man, I'm just trying to help."

"You need to do better."

Braden thought I worked for the government, but I was just doing this because it was the right thing to do, and I'd been funding the entire family's existence for the last four months. After he calmed down, I discovered that Braden had never worked with my guy. Fardeen, Wafa's brother, had been Braden's interpreter and risked his life many times when they fought against the Taliban. Braden thought that Fardeen's brother and extended family should get visas, but unfortunately, only immediate family qualified. As far as I could see, Wafa had only worked with Americans for six months, but the minimum requirement was twelve, and I couldn't see any other reason why he might qualify for an SIV.

I called Fardeen, who lived in California, to give him the bad news. "I don't think I can make this happen, man. There just isn't enough justification. I'm sorry."

Fardeen paused in thought, then said, "I might have some information."

"Really? I looked at everything. I was pretty thorough."

He sighed. "Anoosh was on the Presidential Protection Service (PPS) for both Afghan presidents. It's basically the Afghan Secret Service."

"What the fuck? Why didn't he tell me? It would have made everything a whole lot easier." The PPS had a special caveat in the rules to get an SIV. After I hung up, we began building his case, getting photos of Wafa with Presidents Ghani and Karzai, Afghan government IDs, etc. Finally, I felt Wafa might have a chance. It was a solid SIV packet, and I called Fardeen back.

"Listen Ben, our mother has no idea he was part of the protective service," he told me. "He doesn't want her to know. She'd probably kill him."

The brothers both swore me to secrecy; I could never reveal his service to his mother, but that was okay. I finally had enough to get him and his family SIVs.

Jan 28, 2022

Mohammed was compromised.

Somehow, with Mohammad bringing aid to our Afghan families, the Taliban had figured out what he was doing and were sending him threatening text messages. After what happened to our Afghan SOF guy who sent us his last video right before the Taliban cornered and most likely killed him, we were afraid the Taliban might do the same to Mohammad. We had made another friend in the chat rooms, a woman called Granny, who was remotely in contact with a team of Afghan SOF in Kabul led by an Afghan named Superman. Our "Safe Houses" didn't really have any security, they were just places for the at-risk Afghans to stay until we could come up with a plan to get them out of the country. Granny was funding real safe houses, made of solid materials, with armed guards who she called her "superheroes". The people put there couldn't leave for their own safety and the safety of the others in the safe house. She agreed to help hide Mohammad.

Granny coordinated with Superman and decided on a date and time. On the specified date, we were out of contact with Mohammad for three hours, and Jess paced the house in worry. This kid, 23 years old, had lost his fiancé, his country, and now was being taken away from the city he grew up in to be placed under house arrest, all because he had helped us. Suddenly, her phone dinged. A message from Mohammad.

"Sister, I am safe, but I have no clothes. I have nothing."

After that, we didn't want to risk anyone else taking supplies to the families. The Afghans we had been housing in Kabul and Mazar were losing hope. Many returned to their homes to see if they could exist under the radar of the Taliban, and we started closing down our safe houses.

Afghanistan would always be on our mind and in our hearts after everything we'd been through and seen, but the reality was becoming clearer every day. It would be impossible to financially maintain those safe houses indefinitely. The sprint of getting people into the gates during the evacuation was over, and the middle-distance races to hide people in Mazar in hopes of getting them a flight out was coming to an end. We weren't giving up, but we needed to plan for the marathon now, a new long-term strategy. If they didn't qualify for a U.S. SIV, then we needed to find countries that were willing to support Afghan refugees, which was a better use for the money.

As Duke, a friend of ours from the chat rooms, once said, "we were trying to solve an Uncle Sam-size problem with the personal checking accounts of veterans." And that checking account didn't have an unlimited supply of money.

Feb 12, 2022

"You should go, Ben," said Travis Peterson. I met him in the chat rooms during the evacuation, and now he was a founder of the Moral Compass Federation. "You're responsible for a lot of Afghans surviving the evacuation. It will give you some closure. You'll be able to see the fruits of your labor, so to speak."

He was talking about the one hundred fifty plus Afghans who were being resettled in Houston, Texas, many of whom Jess and I had guided through Abbey or Black gate, and others we'd housed in Mazar.

The YMCA was the resettling organization in Houston. They had unfurnished apartments already rented for the refugees and some furnishings located in a warehouse, but they were extremely undermanned. Jess and I flew in, joined by Deaton, Jess' brother Brandon, Travis, and a few others I knew only from the chat room until that point. The YMCA had blankets, pillows, pads, and tampons, but not many vehicles to transport supplies. Each of us was given a list of ten families and phone numbers with notes like: no English, speaks a little English, severe combat trauma, bad PTSD, etc.

Jess and I rented a U-Haul and started dispersing the YMCA items, buying food, delivering used furniture, and helping in any way we could. Many of the Afghans were grateful and appreciative, inviting Jess and me over for dinner, which is how we met Fawad and his family. His family had gotten out through Abbey gate with the help of another organization. During dinner one night, he told me about his sister, who had escaped to Mazar-i-Sharif after the last U.S. plane left in Kabul and then was able to catch a flight with Task Force Argo to Kiev, Ukraine.

"I got her on that plane!", Jess exclaimed. "We had her in one of our safe houses. I remember because she was pregnant, which was one of our priorities, and I arranged for her transport to the airport. We were really lucky Argo had room." Fawad expressed his appreciation and got on a video call with her so she could thank us, too.

Travis and I reached out to our community on social media to find employers for the Afghans—people who liked to think outside the box, take risks, and were willing to give these families a chance. A bounty hunter named Steve Tidwell interviewed a number of them to join his business. Almost all the Afghans were from elite military units, so they knew their way around guns and had experience with violent situations.

Fawad signed up to work with Tidwell as a bounty hunter soon after we returned to Atlanta and assisted in the capture of a child predator on his first day of work. That was icing on the cake for us. We had saved people in need only to have them, in turn, help other people. It was really amazing to be in the middle of God's plan and see it so clearly being implemented.

We eased the lives of dozens of families during the week we were there, and Travis was right. It was cathartic to see some of the people we had worked with reach the proverbial finish line and start their lives again. It would not be easy for them, but at least they had a chance now. Overall, the work in Houston was backbreaking and exhausting, but it filled our souls and left us motivated to drive on. Some of the footage from Houston and interviews with Jess and I ended up being broadcast in Afghanistan, Saudi Arabia, and Qatar, with voiceovers in Dari and Farsi, which started up a fresh inundation of aid requests. WhatsApp and Signal were blowing up 24/7.

Feb 24, 2022

My phone rang at zero-dark-thirty a couple of weeks later. It was Josh Jenkins.

"Can you get me to Ukraine? I want to help."

"What the hell are you talking about?"

"I'm an expert in demining. They're going to need that over there."

While I'd been sleeping, Russia had invaded Ukraine. One of the goals of Flanders Fields, besides helping Veterans get help for substance abuse, was to assist them to get back on their feet and find purpose. Josh thought he would find purpose in the battle zone. I immediately began raising money for Josh's trip, including equipment he would need to train Ukrainians in bomb disposal.

Meanwhile, Brian Stern, another of my chat room buddies, and Travis hit me up over the next few days, asking if I could assist them with finding safe routes out of Ukraine for fleeing refugees. I let Jessica take complete charge of the Afghan safe house shutdown while I focused on this new problem. There wasn't much I could add to the information they already had, as the government and the UN were controlling the situation as best they could, but I suddenly became a focal point for connecting people.

Fawad called me three days after the invasion. "Ben, please help my sister." She had barely gotten settled before the war started. Now, at eight months pregnant, she was fleeing for her life again. I connected her with Brian, who was already on the ground with routes and intelligence. Initially, the plan was to move her to the Romanian border, where all the non-Ukrainian citizens were being directed. Unfortunately, the border entry points were backed up, and she went into labor. She then rushed to the Polish border. We lost touch with her and weren't sure what happened until Fawad sent us a photo the next day of her nursing her baby, who had been delivered in a Polish hospital.

Larry Provost, another chat buddy, had adopted a Ukrainian baby years before from an orphanage, and he asked me to help the orphanage director get her orphans to safety. I spoke to her on video through WhatsApp. They'd already lost power, and I could hear the air raid sirens screaming in the background. The reality was that I had no capability in Ukraine, but I was a person who knew other people. I connected her with Brian to see if he had any assets to help her and the children, but there was nothing else I could do. It broke my heart that I had nothing more to offer her.

This had been the nature of our lives for the last year and a half. Ever since the evacuation of Afghanistan, we seemed to stumble into people in need. Then, we'd use the unique skills we had learned as addicts to solve problems, connect people, and raise money if needed. Sometimes, like in the case of Fawad's sister, it was a happy ending. Sometimes, like the case of the Ukraine orphans, we never found out what happened to them. We prayed for them, that they made it to safety and didn't need our help anymore, but we had to move on. There were always more people to help. Onto the next problem.

Mar 12, 2022

"You sure this is what you want?", I asked Jess as we approached the tents. In addition to solving problems in Ukraine and Afghanistan, we were still trying to work through the red tape to get houses from the Chattanooga authorities to create halfway houses.

After spending the day checking properties on the housing list given to us by Chattanooga's mayor's office, we were now visiting homeless camps. It was freezing, somewhere in the teens, and we'd spent most of the day in the car. Now though, we approached on foot, trying not to slip. It had snowed recently, and the ground was a sloshy mess.

"I don't want you to buy anything for my birthday," she told me. "I just want to spend the money on food and other stuff for those that need it here."

We were armed with bags of chips, nutrition bars, flavored soft drinks purchased from Costco, and cartons of Newport cigarettes from a gas station we passed on our way over. Some people came up to us knowing we had handouts, and others didn't want anything to do with us. It didn't hurt our feelings, we just wanted to help.

When the crowd cleared, we started going tent to tent, slapping on the side to make ourselves known. Overall, we covered three camps that night, and when we got back to the hotel, we had to thaw out our fingers and toes.

Most people who came to help only brought clothes, blankets, food, and sometimes coffee, but nobody brought cigarettes unless they've lived the experience of being homeless. It's instant trust. It's currency.

The next day, we came back to the camps after checking out more houses on the mayor's foreclosure list. We spent three hundred dollars on dollar menu items from McDonalds and bought more Newports. Within fifteen minutes of our arrival, women in the camps went back to turning tricks and others started smoking crack in front of us. That's what trust looks like in that environment.

I don't know that anyone decided to get treatment as a result of our visit, but we were there in the snow with those people, showing them we'd been there and they could do better if they wanted to take the first step.

That was our first foray into street outreach.

That night, we discussed what we'd seen. Hundreds of people who needed help getting off the street, most of them not veterans.

"I don't want to step over anyone that needs help just because they aren't vets," said Jessica.

I agreed. Flanders Fields didn't hit the core of who we wanted to help. It was too restrictive. While it had been convenient for helping the Afghan vets, we weren't going to be able to impact the street addicts. Our calling was bigger than only the veterans.

Bryan Owens, Judge Dwyer, Ben Owen, Jessica Owen, and Robert Coleman after the meeting about buying Rebos.

We were aired on a news station in Afghanistan after the resettlement work we did.

The Afghan resettlement crew at the YMCA in Houston, Tx

Searching properties in Chattanooga.(We really wanted this old firehouse.)

Fawad - as we all eat dinner together.

WE FIGHT MONSTERS

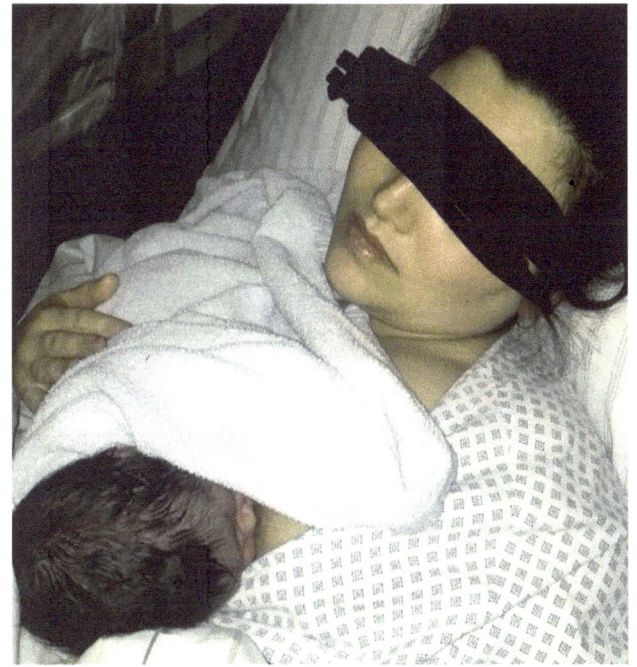

Fawad's sister after giving birth in Poland.

Chattanooga homeless camp - Jessica's birthday 3/12/2022

Chattanooga homeless camp - Jessica's birthday 3/12/2022

CHAPTER THIRTEEN
UVALDE

APRIL 2022

"I GUESS WE'RE ONE HUNDRED PERCENT INVESTED IN REBOS now, baby girl," I told Jessica, putting down the phone. "The mayor of Chattanooga no longer needs our help. They think it's a great idea, and they're going to contract it out instead of letting us do it."

"Fuck them," said Jessica. "But I also wish them success."

It was all good because our hearts were in Memphis, anyway. We weren't raising nearly enough money to buy Rebos, but we weren't going to quit either. Chattanooga had been low-hanging fruit because we had hoped the mayor would give us free houses to start our halfway house project. But it wasn't all wasted time. Helping at the homeless camps had made us aware that we needed to do something beyond helping the veterans, and we started brainstorming how to help all the addicts.

It was a monster of a problem, and we felt that we had a unique insight. We just had to figure out how to attack it in a way that other non-profits weren't already addressing.

In the meantime, I was taking off to help with another Afghan issue. Three sources in the chat room had mentioned that there were twenty-two thousand Ukrainian refugees in Tijuana, Mexico. Some warned that they were being trafficked and that most of them were women and children. I couldn't find anyone who had ground truth, so I took it upon myself to figure it out. While I was concerned about the trafficking aspect, if that was true, what initially interested me was how Ukrainians were getting visas to Mexico, and if I could use the same process to help our displaced Afghans.

Fortunately, I didn't need a passport because that problem still hadn't been solved. I just drove across the border. There wasn't even a checkpoint to get in. When I arrived in Tijuana, I discovered the trafficking rumor was bullshit. There was an organization supported by Mila Kunis and Ashton Kucher that waded through the red tape to get the Ukrainian refugees into Mexico with additional aid to apply for visas to the U.S. This was great news because it meant that I could focus on the task of helping Afghans.

I connected with Duke, the founder of Operation North Star, and his interpreters, and we visited the other refugee camps nearby. Most of them were for people from South American countries in search of a better life. Where the Ukrainian camp was clean, organized, and the people were well fed, that wasn't what I found in the other camps. There was little support for these camps, not much food, and many health problems. Where the Ukrainians were standing by for visas, these people only had hope in the Coyotes, cartel members who specialized in human trafficking and smuggling. Their dangerous journeys were far from over. Seeing the quality of life these people suffered through, I truly began to understand the effect that the U.S. border policies were having. It was promising a new life of prosperity, but mostly delivering death, rape, human trafficking, or robbery at the hands of Coyotes and Mexican cartels.

The local attitude towards the comparatively luxurious accommodations for the Ukrainians was made quickly apparent, as a dead body with hands and feet bound with duct tape was left outside the camp on the day we arrived. At first, we believed this hatred was reserved for the white European encampment, but after a visit to a Haitian camp nearby, we learned it was for anyone non-Spanish speaking. The Haitian camp was far less crowded, but it certainly didn't have the welcoming atmosphere that the south and central American migrant camps did. As I entered, I was quickly surrounded by an angry mob of men screaming in creole.

"Do you speak creole or French?", I shouted at our interpreter.

"NO!" he shouted back, I could see the fear in his eyes. He was just a kid, the son of a local surgeon.

After a tense few moments, I identified the de facto "leader" of the Haitians and was able to pull him into the middle of the mob with me, which got the crowd to settle down enough to be able to hear each other. He was waving multiple manila envelopes in my face, which I realized were medical documents. With my background in healthcare, and a surgeon's son with me, I saw an opportunity to diffuse the situation. It was clear they were in need of medical help.

We eventually found a Haitian who spoke enough Spanish to communicate with us. We identified all the refugees in need of services, then we brought in some of our newly made friends in the Baja state government to coordinate getting some doctors into the camp. We left the Haitians feeling good that we'd been able to get them the help they needed, but an hour later, I got a call that elements of local organized crime had entered the camp and opened fire, killing around 25 of the 100 or so refugees. Apparently, their angry approach at trying to get the help they needed had already tainted local sentiment towards them.

On our way back to the hotel, a gun truck sped past our caravan and blocked the road. Mexican Nation Guard Soldiers piled out and encircled our vehicles, rifles pointed in our faces, screaming orders in Spanish. Duke was an old Army recon platoon sergeant and nothing phased him.

"I don't know what you're yelling at me for, you're the ones that just fucked up," he told the soldier on his side, grinning and twirling a toothpick between his lips.

I had no idea what his game plan was, but if those ended up being his last words, I gotta give him props for the badassery factor. Fortunately, I don't think that soldier spoke a lick of English.

Our locals, Carlos and Guidel, had gotten out of their vehicle behind us and were talking to the National Guard commander in Spanish. I later found out that they'd gotten the commander to look me up on socials, promising him that I would hook them up with body armor and weapons if they just let us go on our way, which they did without demanding the usual bribes the Mexican NG is famous for when harassing foreigners.

The next day, I made an appointment with the U.S. consulate to discuss the Afghan situation. David was in charge of the Tijuana office of the U.S. State Department and laid everything on the table. "If I can help you with the Ukrainians, let me know how," I told him. "But what I'd really like to do is find a path forward for visas into Mexico for endangered Afghans to wait out their SIV approvals."

"It feels very inhumane that it's taking as long as eight hours to get a humanitarian parole approved for these Ukrainian nationals to get into America," he told me.

That's what was bothering him? It fucking blew my mind. Afghans were still dying eight months later, waiting for SIVs to be approved. South Americans were paying exorbitant amounts of money to be smuggled across the border. And David was unhappy with the eight-hour delay for the Ukrainians?

I explained my efforts since August 2021 with the Afghans, and he was dumbfounded. He had no idea any of that was going on. He seemed to want to help, so we agreed to continue discussing possible solutions for the Afghans while working through our unique communities (his official, mine grassroots). I also expressed my concern about getting back across the border.

"I don't have a passport," I told him.

"It was taken away?"

"No, I've never had one." I then told him about my efforts in Tajikistan and my problem with getting a passport due to my complicated tax situation.

"Well, I should be able to help you there. You're an American trapped abroad. I can issue you a one-year passport."

Fuck yeah!

"I'll get the paperwork done today. Just come by the consulate tomorrow to pick it up. Ask at the American Citizen's Service desk once you get through security."

I was psyched. Finally. If I had a passport, I would be able to help solve problems on the ground internationally instead of by email and phone. Sometimes, a problem just needed someone on the ground who could think outside the box and bring people together to do good things. I felt that was the main reason I had been so ineffective in Ukraine.

The next day, I went to the consulate.

"I'm sorry, I can't issue you a passport," said the lady behind the desk.

"Can I speak to David, please?", I asked politely, my hopes sinking.

He came down to talk to me. "I've never seen anything like this before. I don't know who you pissed off, but the system will not allow me to give you a passport, which is crazy—you're an American. I can literally get known criminals passports back to the US so that agencies can escort them and put them in prison. I put your name in the system, entered that you are trapped abroad, and it won't allow it.

I thanked him for his efforts and promised we'd be in touch to move the Afghan problem forward, then headed to the border to try my luck. I showed my driver's license to the agent. I had notified my friends at Homeland Security of my situation (the ones I'd met in chatrooms in 2021 during the Afghan evacuation) and was fully prepared to be pulled into secondary for an interrogation.

"Passport," asked the border agent.

"I don't have one," I replied.

He glared at me. "What are you doing in Mexico?"

"I'm working on the Afghan evacuation and also helping some of the Ukrainian refugees."

He pointed at my ball cap. "You ATF?"

Some of the Afghans I'd helped in Houston had given me one of their unit patches, ATF, which stood for Afghan Territorial Forces. I just happened to be wearing that hat as I crossed. Realizing there was probably some rivalry between the agencies, I replied, "Oh, ATF, yeah, not our ATF. Fuck those guys."

He laughed. "Alright, well, you're definitely an American. Come on in. Welcome home."

I'd have to thank those guys for getting me out of a sticky situation.

On May 24, 2022, a former student entered Robb Elementary School in Uvalde, Texas, took the lives of nineteen students and two teachers, physically injured at least seventeen others, and left a community of families and friends grief-stricken.

My phone hadn't stopped buzzing from people asking if Flanders Fields was able to assist. I was in Houston, attending an NRA convention for Black Rifle Co. I didn't see how we could get involved since there weren't veterans involved.

The next day, we got a call from Kay, a member of Task Force Argo. We had coordinated things together during the Afghan evacuation. "What are you guys doing about Uvalde?", she asked.

"Our hands are tied. Flanders Fields is directly connected with helping veterans."

"Perfect. There are a lot of vets impacted. I used to be a teacher here. I know a lot of people from that city. Some of the first responders are veterans, and they need counseling. One of the teachers who was killed was the mother of a Marine, who is coming back for the funeral."

"Shit, okay. I had no idea."

"I'm going to put you in contact with my friend Pilar. She's kind of a community leader down there."

Within minutes, I was talking with Pilar, who was a mess. Her five daughters went to a local charter school but played softball with all of the Robb Elementary kids and were close to many of the victims and their parents. Her dad, June, was the funeral director for Uvalde, and he had helped carry the bodies of the children out of the school after the shooting. He told me about what he had seen. "When I finally came home that night and sat beside the pool, I put my feet up, and blood poured out of my shoes."

There was no doubt these people needed help, but was I the right person to give it to them?

I spoke to Jess that night. "I've been asked to go to Uvalde."

"What the fuck for? Don't you think they're more likely to blame you because of your connections to the gun industry?"

I told her about the situation. "If there's anything Flanders can do, then I need to get it done. Some have already asked me, but if they don't want me in the end, then I'll leave."

She was silent for a moment. "I want to go," she finally said. "But I doubt we could find childcare on such short notice. Take Jacob."

"No, absolutely not." There was no way I was taking my sixteen-year-old son. That didn't make sense to me at all. "He doesn't need to see that."

"Look baby, you need to focus on the big picture, getting help and money where it needs to go. Helping the parents cope. If I can't be there for the babies, you need somebody to focus on them. Jacob is really good with kids. He can address that. Ultimately, it will do more good for those kids. And he wants to go."

She had some good points; I couldn't do everything myself. "Okay, have Robert bring him. He's buying tickets now." My Black Rifle Co business partner had already told me he wanted to help. "Also, Josh needs more supplies for his training."

In late April 2022, we finally had enough money to send Josh Jenkins to Ukraine. Flanders funded bomb tech bags, EOD kits, and his plane ticket. He had a volunteer job initially with Bomb Tech without Borders to help with humanitarian demining. He was so full of purpose, spearheading the effort to prevent the tragedy of unexploded ordnance hurting or killing innocent men, women, and children. That was a success story in itself. "If we have the money, let's continue to support him. It's the best success story: us supporting people who do great things." She agreed. For now, I needed to concentrate on problem-solving in Uvalde.

The next morning, I briefly attended the NRA conference before starting the drive from Houston to Uvalde. Predictably, there were protests outside blaming guns for the shooting. I was there to conduct business for Black Rifle Co, but I was honestly questioning my part in the gun industry. While I didn't blame guns, and I would always carry one myself, I wasn't sure I wanted to do that for a living anymore; it just didn't represent who I was.

Pilar had been busy on social media ever since we spoke. There were comments about Flanders Fields coming to help, though I honestly couldn't imagine what help I was going to bring. When I arrived, I drove straight to her dad's house in my rental car, passing the town civic center where the FBI and Red Cross had set up a command center. The place was crawling with cameras. Uvalde is a small rural town, and there were lots of "Trump For President" signs still visible in many of the yards.

As I approached June's house, I began to second-guess myself. I didn't want to go. There was nothing on this Earth that fucked me up worse than seeing kids suffer. I was scared shitless. I stopped in front of the house to gather my thoughts, when suddenly I was swarmed by a gaggle of kids tapping on the windows, laughing, and giggling. They grabbed my hands and dragged me around back to introduce me to their grandpa, June. I immediately felt welcome. There were lots of hugging and smiles, everyone thanking me profusely for coming. All I could think was, "Dude, I haven't done anything."

There was an endless amount of food prepared, and we spent the next three hours talking about life and eating, just getting to know each other, before we even brought up the reason I was there. By then it was just June and Pilar's husband, Fred, a combat veteran and Border Patrol Agent. They spoke about the community's reaction, and the invasion of the press. The consensus was that no one wanted the event to be blamed on gun violence. It was the work of a mentally unstable individual. The general fear was that the press would make a political statement about guns and distract from what actually happened and the mourning of the families involved. As I listened to them speak, I saw the crimson stains beside the pool, now dried—the blood that had poured from June's shoes. The blood of innocents.

What am I doing here? How could I possibly help?

I didn't sleep well that night.

I felt lost in my business, my life, and my purpose.

I spent the night in an Airbnb that Kay's mom owned, which was good because every possible place to stay was filled with the press. Two friends of Ka's—Gia, a trauma therapist, and her husband Eric, a

Homeland Security Investigations Agent—had shown up late that night and were staying in the same place. Robert and my son, Jacob, arrived early that afternoon. More volunteers had messaged they would come, but for now, it was just us five. We all met at June's funeral home to discuss how my team could help.

"Pilar and I have spoken to the community leaders," began June. "We think that the best thing would be to keep the media out of our business. Prevent them from disrupting the services at the funeral home and at the funerals as well."

I nodded. "We'll help where we can."

"The funerals aren't going to start for a few days," said Pilar. "In the meantime, I want to take you to visit the families."

I can't do this. I'm not ready to look into the eyes of grieving parents who have just lost a child. Despite those thoughts, I started giving out instructions to my team. "We'll need care packages for the kids. Jacob, take charge of that. We'll go shopping as soon as we leave here. When we arrive, after the introductions, Gia focuses on the women, Jacob will get with the kids, and I'll talk with the men."

I still wasn't comfortable, but if this was what Pilar and June thought the people needed, I could be there for them.

"One more thing," said Pilar. "The Red Cross and the FBI reached out to me to have you call them at the command center in the Civic Center."

"What the hell for?", I asked as my team headed toward the cars.

"I think they want you to convince the families to talk with them. They probably think the community trusts you because I've been talking you up on social media the last couple of days."

I shook my head. "That place is crawling with journalists. If the families wanted to go there, they would have gone. I don't see any reason to get involved in that. Making sure these families' needs are taken care of by people that give a shit is the most important thing right now."

I'd be damned if I helped make this a political fiasco when all these people needed was to heal.

When we entered Steve's living room, he was lying face up on a tattoo chair in his underwear with someone drawing his daughter's face on his right arm. Elena had been killed by the shooter. His mother and sister had greeted me with big hugs and tears before going to the kitchen with Gia. Steve was a big 'ole Hispanic man, and once he saw my tattoos, we got into a comfortable conversation about their meaning. The tattoo artist had come all the way over from San Antonio with his chair and ink.

"Steve, if there is anything I..."

"You're here, man. You're here, and that's enough."

With Pilar, we made the rounds throughout the day and the next, visiting families. Most were welcoming. A few weren't, but that was okay, too. It was a very broken and raw community that blamed the local police force for what had happened and was already tired of the press. It was a miracle that more violence hadn't erupted since the shooting.

Two days after I arrived, the funerals began. By this time, other veterans who had been helped by Flanders Fields had seen my posts on social media and came to town, making us eight strong. The news media were lined up around June's funeral home. The Uvalde Police Department was notably absent, with the Texas DPS and other nearby police departments picking up their slack. Unfortunately, the police couldn't prevent the press from filming, but my team made every effort to disrupt their shots. It was reprehensible, freelancers trying to get shots of little kids crying so hard they were vomiting and families who just wanted to be left alone. At one point, I snatched a cell phone from the hands of a journalist who had snuck in under the guise of being a mourner.

I was so proud of my son, who continued to block cameras with his body. "I get paid to be here, kid," one cameraman told him. "I can do this all day."

"I don't give a fuck, so can I," said Jacob.

The man lowered his camera and Jacob put his crotch square in front of the lens. "And I'm a minor, you pervert."

The man bowed his head and walked away.

I saw some bikers at a gas station across the street and approached them, telling them what was going on and asking if they could help make a human wall. Before I knew it, we had twenty more bodies on the line.

That evening, I started using my social media to inform and ask for help. I directed people to the individual family GoFundMe accounts, hoping they would receive financial assistance in their time of need. At one point, some Afghan followers sent me a video of them holding a prayer circle for the Uvalde children and their families.

Most of the journalists weren't that bad. They told me they didn't want to be there, but it was their job. I told them they didn't need to show the faces of children to do their jobs. And they didn't have to be so inhumane.

At the end of the first day, my team stopped by the only Starbucks in town, and it was packed with more press, every single table full. I saw one guy from the Associated Press who had a printer, his computer, and three bags on a six-person table. I was so angry that I went on Facebook Live. "Look at this jackass!" I ranted, showing the man's equipment and face. "These guys have no respect for the families that are in pain." He gathered his things up and left, as did others when I wandered around the store reporting on the reporters. The employees gave my team free coffee for the rest of the time we were in town. They were fed up with the demanding and mostly impolite visitors.

After that day, more and more members of multiple motorcycle gangs from Thin Blue Line LEMC, Marines MC, Guardians of the Children, Bandidos, and more showed up until we had a couple of hundred bikers showing up for each funeral, which made national news. The bikers blocked cameras with their bodies, demanding that journalists stay on the sidewalk and off the funeral home property to allow the families their privacy. The whole community was understandably emotional about everything, and I think if we didn't have their help and the press had been allowed to go unchecked, the people of Uvalde would have taken all their stress out on the press.

On day four, a place called Ox Ranch, which was about forty-five minutes outside town, offered me and my team a place to stay. Kay's mom had a previous reservation and there was nowhere in town to stay, so it was serendipitous that they called. Ox Ranch was a big game hunting preserve, and they were awesome hosts. My team changed as time went on, Jacob having to return to school and other veterans showing up to help over the following ten days.

The final funeral was for a teacher who had been married to a Uvalde cop, and it was the only event that the local police force showed up for. They formed up in a group under the shade of one of the only trees at the cemetery. This pissed me off because there were tons of women and kids braving the one-hundred-plus degree heat.

"No problem for them to take cover now," said one of the Texas DPS agents standing beside me as we watched them.

At the end of the ceremony, a bunch of white doves were released, and almost simultaneously, a dozen or more black crows took flight from the shade tree over the Uvalde cops. I felt goosebumps. It was an ominous moment, and there was total silence from the crowd.

Tijuana migrant camp. (Conditions were poor, outside. Open sewage kids had to navigate around)

Ben, kids, and Interpreter in Tijuana migrant camp.

Ben and Duke - Tijuana migrant camp

Ben - Haitian migrant camp

Ben - Tijuana migrant camp (There were about 300 kids inside this open space with only 2 adults to supervise)

Ben- Tijuana migrant camp

Haitian migrant camp - raw sewage and trash everywhere

Ben and interpreter trying to diffuse the situation with angry Haitians.

Situation diffused - Ben in the middle

Ben - Haitian migrant camp

Inside Ukrainian camp - nice, organized, plenty of toys and adult supervision.

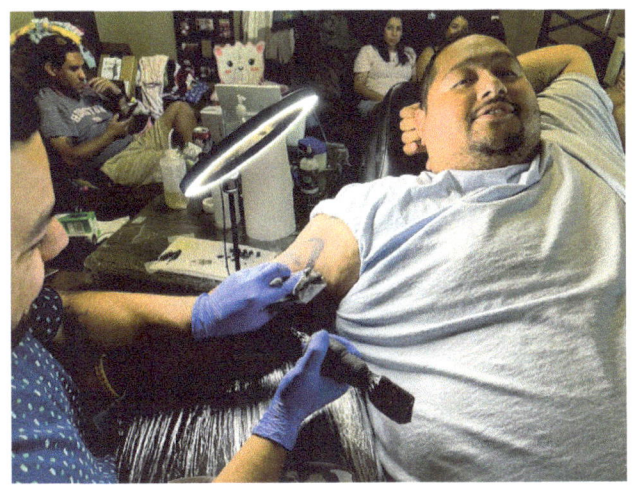

Steve getting the tattoo of Elena

Picture of Elena used for Steve's tattoo

Jacon keeping kids happy

WE FIGHT MONSTERS

Jacob playing with kids to keep their minds off of the shooting.

Ben, gathering Banditos to help cover the funerals so the media can't get footage.

Ben and Jess Robb Elementary

Robb Elementary

Ben, Jess, and Pilar

CHAPTER FOURTEEN

REBOS

NOVEMBER 2022

"Fuck this shit," said Matt, suddenly leaping to his feet and pointing at me. "Fuck you." He pointed at Jess. "Fuck her." Then he walked out of the room and out of the house.

In a way, it was funny, because everyone in the house, including Matt, had bitched consistently about the way Tony and Stephanie Shelby had run Rebos. But they didn't know us at all, so they were pissed.

I can't say it was unexpected. When you live in a halfway house, your life is dictated by the people who run it. Your sobriety, your recovery, every single thing you have is at their mercy. Also, addicts hate change; it's one of their least favorite words on earth, coming in only behind the word "no". They want to be in control of every motherfucking thing. They would rather have something they know and understand, yet dislike, than something unknown that might be better. So Jess and I knew we were going to be hated because we were new and unknown. Trust was important. We didn't have that trust yet. We'd have to earn it.

After we signed the paperwork, Tony took us over to each of the three houses so we could tell our stories and introduce ourselves to everyone as the new owners. Matt wasn't the only one who wasn't happy. It was all okay, though. I was confident we would win them over. We might not be changing the way things worked from the get go, but we were coming with a completely different attitude.

Tony hadn't tried to make money off Rebos. He had been trying to break even. They were invested in Rebos because it meant something to them, and after looking at their records, I can honestly say they lost money hand over fist most years. I'm sure their endgame was very similar to what actually happened: they mostly broke even on the day-to-day activities, they were helping people in need, and they sold the property at a profit after over twenty years of ownership.

When they had been in charge, everyone who lived there paid to stay except for house managers: tenants paid one hundred and ten dollars per week and senior residents paid fifty-five dollars per week. No one was on salary. If things broke in the house, the rate at which it was repaired was directly related to the item's impact on making the house livable. Instead of curtains or blinds, used sheets covered the windows. The rooms and community kitchens were equipped with cheap furniture and household items that had been donated or were purchased from Goodwill.

It was immediately apparent that we didn't know what we were doing. After all, we were just off the streets ourselves three years earlier. We were terrified, but we had a different vision of Rebos, and no idea if it would work, but we were willing to dedicate one hundred percent of our time and energy to trying.

Vets and victims of human trafficking lived for free, that was really the only major change we made to the Shelbys model. Since Jess and I still lived in Atlanta, and there were periods of time I wouldn't be present, I paid the house managers a salary to run the houses, and I paid a Housing Director to help the individual house managers and report to me. We also began to upgrade the accommodations.

Additionally, Tony had run Rebos like it was still 1993 and computers didn't exist. Documents were shoved in filing cabinets, and keeping them in chronological and alphabetical order seemed to have been a crapshoot at best. The drug tests weren't the most accurate on the market. Fixing these issues joined the list of our first changes.

Tony still lived in the Memphis area and was always around to advise, so we spoke often.

"You're never going to break even if you keep running it like this, Ben," he told me after one of our discussions over a burger at Hueys (home to the world famous Huey burger). "Trust me, I ran that place for twenty years, and I understand the finances inside and out."

"I hear you, man," I replied between bites of my burger. "But I don't plan on making money, I actually plan on losing."

He just couldn't wrap his head around our vision.

Jess and I decided from the beginning that the purpose of the Rebos project was to help addicts get off drugs, off the street, and give them hope. To do that, we couldn't run it with an eye to making money or even breaking even. Without us living in Memphis to do the role of the Director on-site, there was no way to make it a zero sum game.. We had to meet people where they were, show empathy and understanding, and just do the right thing. And if the right and left columns in the accounting book didn't balance, well, that was why we had the non-profits.

The people in Rebos mostly came from drug court, just like I had not too long ago. While there were people like me—people from stable, upper-middle class, two-parent households with professions—most of our tenants were what you would expect. They didn't have a father, and many of them had been on the street since they were teens. Several grew up in foster care. They included criminals, orphans, abused wives, and trafficked teenagers, just to name a few.

Their first forty-five days were paid for by the Drug Court Foundation, and we did our best to use that time to invest in them and their futures, hoping to help get their feet on the ground. Our job was to make them into adults by teaching them life skills that would help them live and thrive in society. With so many who had grown up on the streets and without proper parents, they rarely understood the basics of adulthood or living a productive life.

Once the drug court sent someone to Rebos, we gave them an initial drug screening, then gave them two weeks to find a job. If they were trying, the house manager could extend that two weeks depending on the situation.

The rules could be a culture shock to our tenants, many of whom had lived their entire lives without rules or accountability. To an outsider, some of them might seem absurd or overly rigid, such as requiring tenants to make their beds, or having consequences for stealing a piece of bread from another tenant. But Tony's rules—most of which we kept—had evolved through learning the hard way. If we overlooked minor infractions, bigger problems inevitably developed later. And if we couldn't impart the importance of following simple rules, how could they live in a society that was based on rules in everything they did?

Everyone was required to attend thirty AA meetings in thirty days. After that, they had to attend five meetings a week. We administered random drug screenings regularly, and if a resident failed, they were out. If they wanted to come back, they were required to attend a twenty-eight-day treatment program, which we would coordinate at no cost to them through our non-profit, *We Fight Monsters*. We were willing to pour money and energy into people who we saw trying to better themselves.

After that, we depended on hope and prayer.

NOVEMBER 2022

Once we decided to pay our house and chief managers salaries, we assessed the current managers to determine if we could work well with them and if they were capable of doing business the way we wanted it done. Historically, house managers and senior residents (the manager's assistant) were chosen from those living in the Rebos houses, and we didn't plan on changing that tradition at all. Having lived there myself, I felt it was important to have gone through that experience in order to have the compassion, consistency of treatment, and strength to do the right thing for those passing through Rebos. However, we also wanted to elevate everyone there by creating circumstances for them to evolve beyond Rebos.

Tiffany ran the women's house, fourteen beds. Just putting her on salary wasn't enough to convince her that we were going to do a good job. We would have to prove ourselves to her, put our money where our mouth was, so to speak. I had been on drug court with her at one time, though I didn't have any solid memories of her—probably because of all the dope I was doing. When she heard Jess and I were taking over, she just about quit right then. The salary kept her on a bit longer, but she wasn't convinced we were going to be a positive change until a couple months later when she called me in distress on November 19, 2022.

"The FBI is calling, but I don't want to answer," she told me.

"Look, Tiffany, we've been over this. It's the right thing to do. You're in recovery, and you have to talk to them."

She had been in the middle of a murder trial ever since her boyfriend was shot full of holes and died in her arms. The feds wanted to know what she knew, maybe even use her as a witness, but she was afraid of being a snitch. I had walked her through the idea that she would be helping to make sure other people didn't have to suffer like she did if the feds actually were able to put this guy behind bars.

"Okay, okay. I'll do it." She hung up, only to call me back within minutes.

"How did it go?" I asked.

All I heard was crying on the other side.

"Tiffany, are you alright? What's wrong?"

She sniffed, and I could tell she was trying to compose herself. "It's my sister. She was killed last night in Colorado Springs." She went on to explain that the call hadn't been about the murder at all.

That morning I had seen on the news that there had been a shooting at a gay club there. For some reason, I just knew that I would be drawn into that event, though it made no sense at the time. In my heart, I just had a feeling.

"Tiffany, listen to me. Whatever you need from me, I'm there."

"I don't know how to handle this," she said through sobs. "I don't know how to deal with this. I'm her only living relative that gave a fuck about her. Can you go to Colorado with me?"

"Done," was all I said.

On November 28th, we flew to Colorado. I helped her through the funeral. The authorities had questions for her, and I sat through that with her. Over lunch, Tiffany wondered if something like Rebos would benefit the people of Colorado Springs, and I told her I'd help her figure that out if it was something she wanted to do. From then on, our relationship changed. She realized that when Jess and I say we're family, we really meant it. When we say we got you, we got you for life; it doesn't matter how much it costs us, we'll find a way.

After assessing the other housing managers, we made some changes, but eventually Matt, the guy who stormed out the day we took over, drew our attention. He had had a string of bad luck before we ever met him. He'd spent a lot of time in prison, then married a stripper who he put through college. She became a psychologist, then got cancer and died. The pain of losing her was too much, and he burned his whole life to the ground with drugs and alcohol. He was ordered to serve his entire six-year probation at Rebos, which made him angry as hell. After we took over, that obviously made him more mad. After observing him for a few months, we asked him if he wouldn't mind being a Senior Resident. He prayed on it and spoke with his sponsor, then agreed. Soon after, we promoted him to house manager.

For our Housing Director, we initially chose Bubba. A fifty-seven-year-old balding former Hell's Angel who had done time in the penitentiary. He had been a close friend of Brandon Kelly and myself back in our drug court days. We had even been in Rebos together, before I got kicked out for relapsing. Bubba had been so upset that he packed his stuff up and slept under a bridge that night in protest. That's loyalty.

He had even helped Tony get sober at one time, and had gotten clean himself in 2017. After selling Vinyl siding during the day, Bubba had been helping out for free at Rebos for years. He was super passionate about getting people straight, and he was positive that the whole thing would fall apart if he didn't stick around. For that, Tony had paid his cell phone bill. I recognized his loyalty to the program and me, so I thought he would be perfect as my number two man in Memphis. The goal of Rebos was always to help people evolve into something more, sometimes into something they couldn't even imagine for themselves. After about six months, we offered to use *We Fight Monsters* to pay for him to become a Recovery Coach and a Certified Peer Recovery Specialist, and then got him into school to become a Licensed Alcohol and Drug Addiction Counselor. Bubba had never even graduated high school, and it wasn't easy, but he's sticking it out and passing all of his classes . Meanwhile, we promoted Matt to Men's Housing Director.

Our goal was to always choose the best—people who had been through it all, had empathy, would fight for the other residents, and never lie to us. Amazingly enough, those people rose to the top, and we soon had rock solid management.

Stephanie and Tony Shelby /Ben and Jess Owen - Rebos officially being handed over

Ben goes to Colorado to be there for Tiffany after the Q Club massacre.

CHAPTER FIFTEEN
WE FIGHT MONSTERS

JANUARY 2023

ON JANUARY 26, 2023, I FINALLY GOT UP ENOUGH NERVE TO get out of my car in front of the Melrose Street trap house. It looked deserted. Obviously, Memphis PD had just hit it and shut it down again. It happened all the time.

"Ben? Is that you?"

It was a familiar voice. I turned. "Red?" I asked.

Red. Miss Texas's sister. We had been through some times, and she had always looked out for me and mine. I gave her a big hug and told her what I was doing and why I was there.

"Miss Texas?", I asked her, hoping for some good news.

"Ah, Ben, she had a stroke a while back, but she's a tough old girl. It didn't kill her. She went back to Texas."

"She was always kind. I'd like to talk with her. Do you have her number?"

Red called her right then, and it was good to hear her voice. Miss Texas told us that she had recovered from her stroke and was sober. It warmed my heart.

"If you need anything, you call me," I told her.

"Thanks, white boy, I will."

After we hung up, I turned back to the business at hand. "What's up with the trap?", I asked Red.

"Yeah, it's been shut down for a while, though there's still some using it to store parts from boosted cars."

Something possessed me then, and I walked up to the house and began ripping off the boards. Soon, I had enough space to slip inside and look around.

The first thing I saw was the name "Rodney" painted on the wall in a nice script. Rodney had owned nearly this entire block at one time—fourteen of the seventeen houses. He'd been shot at the back entrance of this place in a robbery gone bad, and the familiar stain on the floor was his blood. As I walked through rooms and hallways, memories came back of the time I had wasted there, and I felt an intense need to buy it, to change it from a place of despair into one of hope. For some reason, I felt that this place was meant to be ours.

"I wanted to meet you, but I am really impressed with what you are doing."

I found the owner of the Melrose house thanks to my social media contacts. Two friends of mine happened to have real estate licenses in Tennessee and reached out to her. In less than a week, I was sitting in front of Chelsea and her dad, Mark.

"We talked about it," Mark continued. "Chelsea and I want to give you the house for free."

I was stunned. "Are you shitting me right now, sir?"

He smiled. "Nope, it's yours. I'll use it as a tax write-off. In fact, I have a real estate lawyer who'll handle everything at no cost."

I could barely speak. "Oh my God, thanks so much!"

I didn't have any money to put into the house once I owned it, so I told the story all over my social media and raised over fifty thousand dollars in six weeks. A few weeks later, I signed for the house and hired some of the guys living at Rebos to help me clean it. Honestly, I had no idea what I was doing, and it was a steep learning curve figuring out permits, a construction dumpster, and the biggest pain of them all—the Memphis Landmarks Commission.

The Commission, a historical society of sorts, claimed the house needed to be restored to its original glory after I'd already demoed most of it. Specifically, they wanted large windows installed and doors replaced. Their requests made no sense, especially since the place was almost falling down when I acquired it. Rodney had previously boarded up windows and doors when he was operating this as a trap house, but the society had never approached him. Once again, I went to social media to bring attention to the problem, and promptly got a call from the mayor telling me I could do the renovations as I please, but to please go through him if I had any future problems.

I had used my following to raise money before, but this was one of the first times that it had changed policy, which wasn't even what I was trying to do. I was just venting.

"We're going to have to shift the timeline for Operation Yellow Brick Road."

Shit.

Jess and I were constantly trying to find innovative ways to get Afghans out of Afghanistan and Pakistan. I had been openly communicating with Travis from the Moral Compass Federation (MCF) about helping the Afghans leave their country for almost a year. MCF had emerged after the evacuation of Afghanistan as a non-profit that brought together a myriad of other nonprofits and funding with the goal of helping Afghans escape the Taliban.

Travis had brought me in on a wild idea back in October 2022. We would try to convince some African countries to accept Afghan refugees with medical training and licenses, mostly doctors and nurses. The plan had been progressing well, with an execution date of April 2023. Today was February 5, and I still didn't have a passport.

The plan was to move the medical personnel to Islamabad, Pakistan, and fly them legally to Victoria Falls, Zimbabwe, on a tourist visa. Then they would be moved by land to the border of South Africa at the Beitbridge Border post and claim asylum. Some of the guys working with Travis had extensive contacts throughout Africa and specifically in South Africa, so they had already contacted lawyers who would meet the refugees at the border to facilitate their movement and address any problems. We all figured it would be easy enough to get asylum due to the need for medical personnel in South Africa. It wasn't a foolproof plan, but we all had a high measure of confidence that it would work.

The emergency that required us to change the dates came about when some Afghan SOF were seriously threatened by the Taliban and needed to leave the country immediately, including Superman and some of the same crew that rescued Mohammad. So, instead of medical personnel, we'd be moving Afghan SOF soldiers and their families. At the time, that seemed like a good idea. That way, we could vet the system with people who were used to rolling with the punches and dealing with any hardships—not that we expected any. Travis immediately got his guys in South Africa working on the Afghans' paperwork for refugee status and communicating with some safari parks that might need additional people to work security.

Personally, traveling to Africa had always been a dream of mine, and I immediately volunteered to meet the Afghans on the ground in Zimbabwe and "shepherd" them to South Africa. Unfortunately, despite my attempts to speed up the process, the State Department was still resisting giving me a passport because of my previous tax situation, even though I had taken care of it already. Travis wanted movement on this within a week.

If I couldn't go, it was imperative to send someone in my stead who was calm under pressure and could think outside the box. Fortunately, I'd been keeping my dad informed about this trip, and he'd mentioned his interest. I felt bad about taking a man who was only ten days away from the freedom of retirement and throwing him into a potentially dangerous situation, but I knew he was equal to the task. Plus, after the mission was complete, he could do some sightseeing. I dialed him up.

"Hey, Dad. I have a proposition for you."

Ben and Red meet for the first time since their active addiction days.

"Rodney" who owned the block and the stain on the floor.

CHAPTER SIXTEEN
AFRICA

FEB 2023

THE UNIVERSE HAD MORE SURPRISES FOR ME.

My dad flew straight to Zimbabwe to meet the other Americans who would help the twenty-three Afghans, of which fourteen were adults and nine were children. He sent me updates frequently. The Afghans were picked up at the airport and taken to a safari lodge for three days while the South African contacts continued to get the legal documents ready to ensure safe passage and a "surprise free" journey.

Honestly, I wasn't worried about the Yellow Brick Road operation. It seemed pretty cut and dry, and I had my hands full trying to raise money for our new projects and still maintain the ones we had. We continued to work on our new house on Melrose when the previous owner, Mark, called. "Hey Ben, I've been following your work on the house. I'd like to give you the house next door, too, if you want it." Everything was happening so fast; it was blowing my mind. We arranged a date when I could sign the paperwork with his lawyer.

My dad continued to send photos, and the operation in Africa seemed to be going according to plan. The lodge even procured a bouncy house and some ponies to keep the kids entertained. They headed for the border in charter buses in the early morning hours of February 16. After receiving a text around midnight Atlanta time confirming they were headed out, I went to sleep.

When I woke up, I saw I had received a text at 3 a.m. saying they had their passports stamped on the Zimbabwe side of the border and they were heading to the South African border check, but there was nothing after that. Slightly concerned, I called.

"Can't talk now. There's been a little misunderstanding. They are accusing us of trafficking the Afghans. I'll call you after I sort this out."

What the hell?

I called Travis, and he was already working on the issue. Apparently, when they switched the travelers from the medical personnel to the soldiers, not all the paperwork was completely done (as we had been assured). Additionally, the lawyers who were supposed to meet them at the border crossing on the South African side were delayed and had lost cell phone coverage. Everyone was safe, but they would probably have to sleep in the bus that night while everything got sorted out. Fortunately, the charter bus drivers had managed to get everyone food and water while they waited.

The next day, I found out that dad's group had been tricked into moving the bus to a "more secure location" during the night, which happened to be on the Zimbabwe side of the border, so they were now under the control of angry Zimbabwean authorities. That evening, they were ordered to leave the charter buses and load onto much smaller immigration buses that didn't have enough seats for everyone, forcing them to sit on each other and in the aisle. My dad continued to update me on the conditions, lack of food and water, and how they forced everyone to use the side of the road as a bathroom. The driver made the ride as uncomfortable as possible, playing music loudly the whole way and turning off the air conditioning.

My dad sent a last text as they arrived at the Zimbabwe Immigration headquarters. I didn't hear anything for a few hours, and I was going crazy with worry. I had just started drifting off to sleep in my living room chair when my phone rang. The clock beside my bed said it was 1 a.m.

"Dad?", I asked sleepily. "Everything alright?"

"Look, these guys are serious, and my phone battery is almost dead, so I'll make this quick. They've given us six hours to figure out how to get out of their country legally or they will deport the Afghans back to Afghanistan and charge the Americans with human trafficking, which carries a minimum sentence of forty years in prison."

I was stunned. "Dad, you need to ask to speak to the US Embassy—"

"Hello?" A strangely accented voice came through my dad's phone. "Listen, you have four hours."

"Who is this?", I asked. "My dad said six hours."

"Well, you now have four. The best option is to have the US take the Afghan refugees in on asylum or find a place where you can go outside Zimbabwe."

The line went dead.

For the last eighteen months, I'd been working on getting Afghans asylum in various countries with little to no success. How was I going to do it in four hours?

I called the US Embassy in Zimbabwe, but they claimed the Americans had broken the law and their hands were tied. I blew up my social media. Even though it was early morning in the US, I had people on multiple continents working on a solution. I called my dad back, and he was allowed to pick up.

"Hey, Dad. I'm not comfortable with this situation. I'm buying you a plane ticket, so just get to the fucking airport and we'll figure out how to help the Afghans. At least you'll be safe."

There was a pause before he replied. "Son, I can't."

"What do you mean?"

"I told you, we've been detained."

"I don't give a fuck. You're an American citizen. Go to the airport."

"Ben, they took our passports."

My heart dropped. He wasn't going anywhere.

Ultimately, Travis connected with someone who had connections in Zambia. With twenty minutes left on the deadline, everyone was granted asylum visas to that country, and we got plane tickets for the next day. I got a text from Dad that said they were heading to the airport where they would spend the night. His phone was almost dead, but he promised to try to call me from there.

Then, for almost eight agonizing hours, I couldn't communicate with him and had no idea what was happening. Finally, my phone lit up with his number.

"Dad, are you alright?"

He laughed. "All our phones were dead, and they wouldn't let us charge them, but one of the Afghans here used a Leatherman tool to dig into the wall, find some wires, and rig up a phone charging station." He then sent some photos of their current accommodations. All of them were locked in three filthy holding cells in the basement of the airport with cockroaches and stained mattresses all over the floor. There was only one working toilet and no sinks for hand washing. The Americans were permitted out to purchase food and water for everyone. Temperatures in the holding cells reached over ninety degrees Fahrenheit, and everyone was drenched in sweat.

Their plane didn't leave until the next evening, but everyone was alive and as healthy as could be expected.

My dad called me back the next day as he was about to board the plane. "You know what that immigration officer told me when he handed me my passport? He said, 'Look, don't let this damage your opinion of Zimbabwe. We'd love to welcome you back to visit one day.'"

"You're bullshitting me, Dad."

"Nope. And I replied, 'I don't think it's on the agenda of my upcoming travel plans.'"

With my dad finally in the clear, I turned my attention back to the block, hiring more workers to accommodate the new house. One of the workers was Drinon, a recovering drug addict who I'd known since 2012. He had given me the ring I used for my wedding with Jess, and we had depended on him to take care of us when we had nothing. He owned a trap house on Woodward and agreed to sell it to me for six thousand dollars. Six months ago, I could barely scrape the downpayment together for Rebos, and now I owned six houses. Also, I was spending so much time in Memphis that I needed a home station. Chelsea had a rental that she gave me for a good price, which allowed me to set up a local operations center.

As I was driving back from the lawyer's office after signing the purchase documents on Drinon's house, I turned up the steep hill on Woodward Street and saw blue lights everywhere. "Fuck, now what?", I said under my breath.

Initially, I thought they had just raided my new purchase, which would make it Shelby County property now. That would suck. In addition to the police cars, there were also a lot of ambulances, which was odd. I drove one block down, parked, and ran through the cut. Good thing I'd run all over this neighborhood trying to escape similar raids in years past.

I approached the house, seeing Tweet's mom screaming. Tweet was the guy who had been dealing out of the house. I was returning to the house to tell him I was the new owner, and he needed to move his business somewhere else.

I headed back to the truck. I didn't need to get in the middle of this. I'd figure out what happened later. Suddenly, a car pulled up behind my truck before I could get in.

"Hey, Ben, come here." It was Mikey, a member of the local mob, and in my opinion, pure evil. He'd once shot Drinon six times for stealing dope and held Jess and me at gunpoint because he suspected we had done the same. I didn't see anything good coming out of talking to him, but he waved me over with the pistol in his hand, and I'd left my own pistol in my truck.

"Get in," he told me.

Shit. I was pretty sure I wasn't going to come out of that car alive, but what choice did I have?

He drove away from the blue lights. "Fucking Tweet," he said. "What a dumbass." As we drove, Mikey confessed. Apparently, two days prior, Tweet had sold some fentanyl to an older couple who had asked for coke, and they overdosed. The woman died, and the man went comatose. The couple were the parents of a member of the Memphis mob, and Mikey had been ordered to put a hit on Tweet. Mikey was confused about how the cops got there so fast, but I knew that the police had put in new stationary cameras facing down the street.

"Mikey stopped the car. Come on."

"Where are we?" I asked.

"This is my crib." He led me into the house.

I immediately started looking for something I could use as a weapon. I knew he had a gun, but I didn't have to give him a second shot. He continued to talk, telling me how he shot Tweet.

"He was coming out of the house, and I just walked up and shot him point blank. Bam!" Mikey took out a beer. "You want something?"

"No." I couldn't find anything that would help me.

"Anyways, he started begging me to call an ambulance, but I just smiled at him and walked away. Man, those cops were there fast." Then, Mikey gave me a tour of his house, showing me two gifts he had bought his daughters. I have no idea why he brought me there. Maybe he just needed to talk it out. After about fifteen minutes, we got back in the car, and he dropped me off by my truck.

"See you, Ben," he said. Then he drove off.

Turns out, Tweet lived. Police raided Mikey's house, and though they couldn't pin the attempted murder on him, they found enough drugs and weapons in his house to violate his parole and put him in prison.

To this day, I don't think I have ever been so scared in my life as when Mikey took me for a ride.

Fila was a pimp. He was also what's known on the street as an Original Gangster or OG. He's sixty years old now, done time for rape and murder, and we used to get high together back in the day. Not now, though. He was becoming a pain in the ass.

After Rodney died, Fila took over managing gang operations and prostitution on the Melrose block. Once he saw me buying property there, he tried to run a mob style protection racket on me. "Pay me or bad things are going to start happening."

I refused and he set my construction dumpster on fire.

He called my phone, but I cut him off. "Look, man, I'm not going anywhere. You can burn down the whole fucking block. I'm not going anywhere."

For some reason, he laid off the intimidation. Maybe he was just getting tired of the racket. Over time, he actually supported us by recommending some of his prostitutes to get detox and rehab help from our non-profits. I don't recommend my methods for solving everything, but I did seem to win some hearts and minds with what I was trying to accomplish. I kept seeing this as a sign that I was doing the right things and heading in the right direction.

Their African domicile

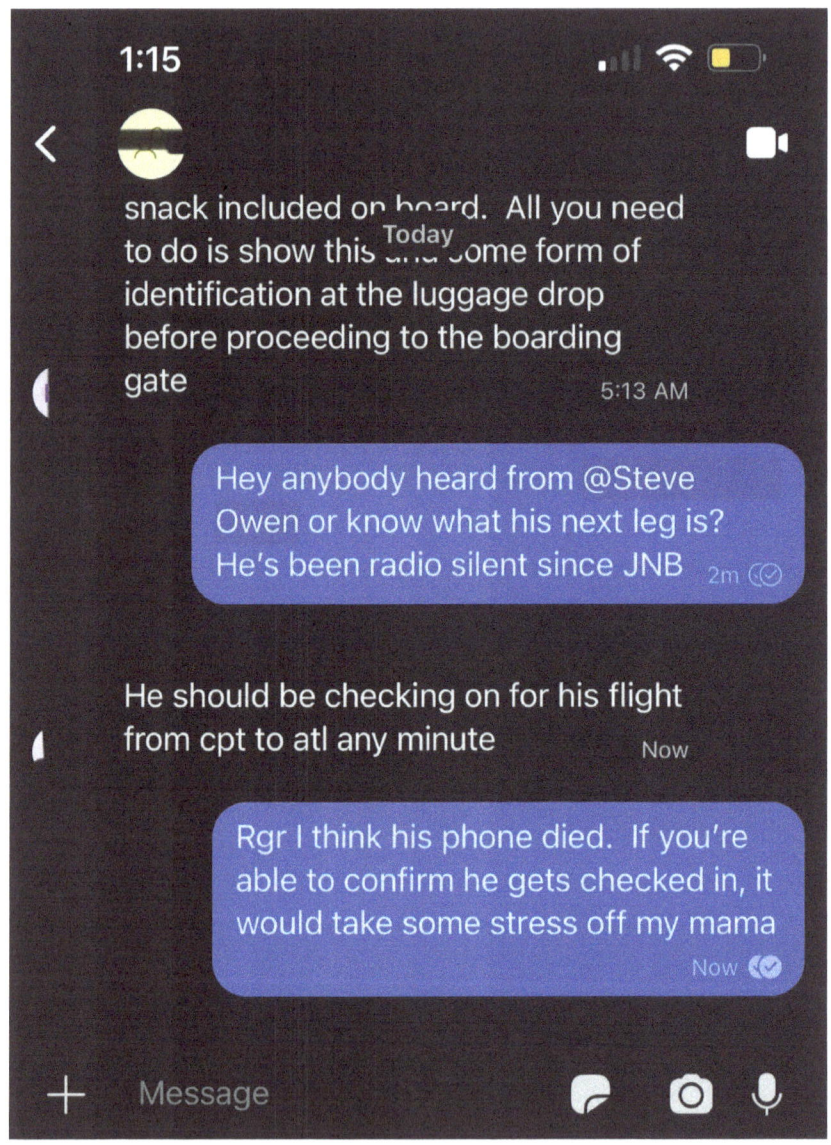

Where's Steve?

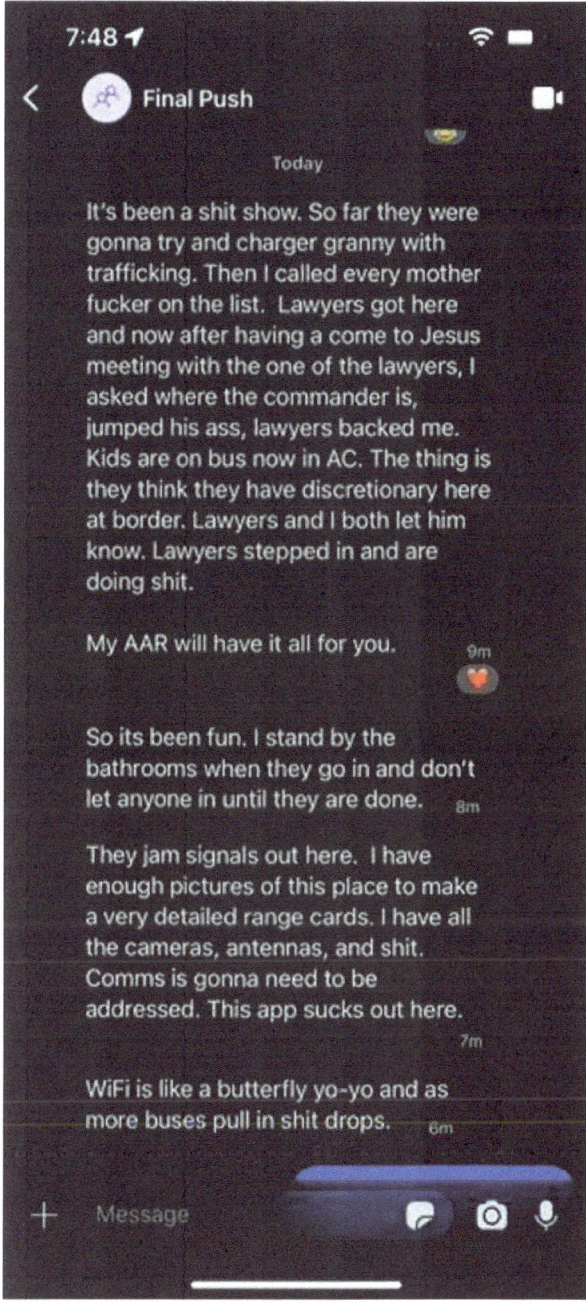

Things starting to get very dicey

Steve Owen with Afghan kids in Africa

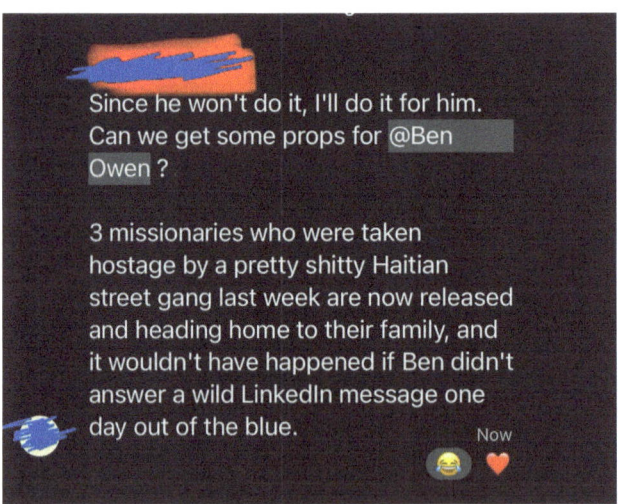

In the middle of getting Steve released, Ben answers a Linked In message and assists in getting 3 hostages released from a Haitian gang.

WE FIGHT MONSTERS

Even the children were locked up

Jonathan Alcocer and Steve Owen on their way back to the USA

Steve Owen- back on American soil, with Melanie Owen

Drinnon sells us 1428 Woodward

Soulsville

Autumn Scott   4 hours ago

MEMPHIS, Tenn. — A man was injured in a shooting in Soulsville Wednesday afternoon.

Memphis Police said officers responded to the shooting in the 1300 block of Woodward Street just after 3 p.m.

The victim was taken to Regional One in critical condition.

Tweet gets shot coming out of Woodward the day we buy it. As the news covers the shooting, Ben is in the background, on his phone, working another evacuation.

CHAPTER SEVENTEEN
CONGRESS

MARCH 2023

IN THE BACK OF MY MIND, I ALWAYS KNEW I'D GET HAULED IN front of Congress one day. Having fired shots across the bow of the Department of Justice, the ATF, the Border Patrol, and many other organizations, I knew it was just a matter of time. It would be for something really, really bad, like bump stocks or forced reset triggers, and it would end with me in jail.

But, shockingly, that's not how it went down. Just before my dad went to Africa, my friend Travis Peterson, founder of Moral Compass Federation, asked me to write a testimony for the chairman of the House Foreign Affairs Committee to be presented at an upcoming congressional hearing concerning the evacuation of Afghanistan.

I wrote up a statement, but I wasn't confident I was the right person. Travis and the other people who were involved were all combat vets with impeccable records, while I had failed out of basic training and my claim to fame was being a crackhead that was able to get good shit done in bad places. It just didn't make sense.

I sent my draft to Scott Mann, who had become a sort of mentor ever since I met him the previous year. His response was, "I wouldn't change a fucking word. It's exactly what they need to hear."

Even though his encouragement boosted my confidence, I just thought it was ludicrous that America fucked up the evacuation of Afghanistan so much and that two crackheads were left to run one of the largest networks of safehouses in Afghanistan. How did we ever get to this point as a civilized nation? How does any of our foreign policy even work? The government talks about "over the horizon" capabilities, but how can they conduct those missions when they can't even manage what is right in front of them?

Despite the fear of embarrassment lurking in the back of my mind, I decided it was the right thing to do if it informed just one person on The Hill. I was very emotional as I sat down for the hearing that occurred on March 8, 2023. Jess was home with the kids watching on C-SPAN. I had just managed to help my dad escape from Africa, where he and the rest of his motley crew were only trying to do what was right, and the U.S. State Department stood by and watched it all happen without lifting a finger when he got arrested. My faith in the U.S. government was at an all-time low.

My testimony was read to the congress, it was submitted as evidence beforehand and I was present in case anyone had any questions. I knew they read it though, because many of them used my exact words to defend their points.

In my testimony, I told about my past with drugs, how I'd dropped out of college and failed out of basic training, and how I had been asked to help with the evacuation. I told about all the efforts and people involved in the evacuation efforts in August 2021, and the efforts of Jess and I to continue keeping people safe afterward after the bomb went off at Abbey Gate on August 26th. I went on to describe the failure of the U.S. government to help America's allies in Afghanistan and the moral injury levied on the veterans who did step forward.

I ended with the following:

> How is it that these things have fallen on my shoulders? Me. A man who, not too many years ago, was homeless, addicted to heroin, in and out of jail, and a raging alcoholic? Do I sound like somebody who

should be responsible for ensuring the safety and security of men holding those secrets? Absolutely not. But here we are.

What's even more egregious is that men and women who are far more than just "barely vets" like myself, men and women who did multiple combat deployments and devoted their entire adult lives to service of our nation, are finding themselves in the same shoes I'm in.

"If not us, then who?"

How true that statement has turned out to be. Nobody is coming, and it's been left up to us. We carry a burden that wasn't ours to bear, but we showed up to bear it, anyway.

We've seen families fall apart, finances destroyed, bankruptcies, divorces, and suicides—all as a direct result of the moral injury created through this disastrous withdrawal. We've also seen more relapses and developing substance abuse issues as a coping mechanism than I care to think about, but it's my calling to deal with that side of things in our veteran population.

My family's long history of military service could well come to an end, as only one of my eight children is currently considering joining, and he's having doubts about it in light of seeing what is happening. Assuming my sons do join, there's an inescapable reality I've come to accept.

My sons will undoubtedly go to war [against] the sons of men I have failed to save, men I was unable to keep alive, and they are many. What better way to radicalize a generation than to convince their fathers to sacrifice their lives in service to our nation and then abandon them to the very enemy we promised to protect them from?

In summary, this was entirely preventable–and can still be mitigated. My faith in the institution of the American Government may have hit an all-time low in 2021, but my faith in the goodness of my fellow Americans has never been higher. As it turns out, in the midst of the greatest calamities suffered by our human condition, we find the greatest people humanity has to offer.

Congress has an opportunity to do the right thing, to mitigate the moral injury affecting an entire generation (or two) of veterans, and honor a promise made to allies and women on the other side of the world. I respectfully request that you take that opportunity and restore America's honor.

I thank the committee for the opportunity to be heard.

My written testimony was admitted to the congressional record by unanimous consent of the House Foreign Affairs Committee.

After the hearing, I was swarmed by the representatives, but they didn't want to talk to me about Afghanistan. They wanted to talk about Memphis.

I never imagined that members of Congress would be taking selfies with me.

They knew I was just a junkie and a drunk. I never hid any of that stuff. Members of Congress from both sides knew my name and were shaking my hand, commenting on how they loved everything I was doing in Memphis.

It was a pivotal moment for me. That was the moment I realized I needed to get even more vocal and laser focused in my messaging.

Ben Owen, Matt Young, Congressman Nunn, Anna Lloyd, and Joe Robert

House Foreign Affairs Committee 1st hearing on Afghanistan (Ben in the back)

Ben and Lt Col (Ret) Scott Mann - the HFAC Hearing on Afghanistan withdrawl

Ben and Congressman Cory Mills- the HFAC Hearing on Afghanistan withdrawl

Ben Owen, Jazz Cannon, and Lt Col (Ret) Scott Mann-the HFAC Hearing on Afghanistan withdrawal

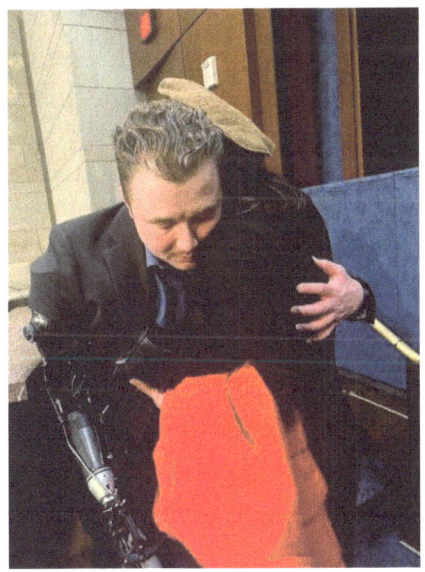

Tyler Vargas-Andrews and Jazz Cannon in an emotional embrace-the HFAC Hearing on Afghanistan withdrawal

CHAPTER EIGHTEEN

GRASSROOTS

Though Jess and I tried to stay true to our calling—helping the addicted in Memphis—I still fell victim to shiny object syndrome from time to time. That inevitably has me running towards fires (sometimes literally) that have nothing to do with the streets of Memphis but still have everything to do with meeting the needs of the suffering.

Scott Mann continued to mentor Jess and me about the power of grassroots movements, working from the bottom up to meet needs when institutional leadership is slow or absent due to the leviathan of bureaucracy. He both invited and inspired us to witness and participate in the miracle of strangers coming together as family and neighbor loving neighbor without regard to race, religion, creed, or politics.

During the Lahaina fire, Scott asked us to get involved. So, Jess and I went boots on ground and sourced albuterol, nebulizers, and medical supplies for the various aid stations around the island, organized relief supplies, and even found a contact to bring AA Big Books and NA Basic Texts to the island.

Then, in 2024, we jumped onboard to help with Hurricane Helene in Western North Carolina after I received a call that first responders in Swannanoa needed Narcan, both for themselves in case of accidental exposure, and for the disaster victims they were serving. I made a few calls, an ad hoc supply chain came together, and next thing I knew, I was on my way to Asheville with 1,200 doses of Narcan.

Part of me ran towards the pain in these disasters because I was compelled to, because it was asked of me, and because it was the right thing to do. But another part of me did it because I had to live it. I had to see it work in real time because I needed to prove to myself beyond a reasonable doubt that these same methods could save the lost on the streets where my wife and I bled.

In between our catastrophe assistance, we saw a lot of change in Memphis. Lucresia is still clean today. We moved her, her fiancé, and two of their grandchildren into the renovated trap house at 1186 Melrose last year.

We permanently closed down an old brothel at 1131 Melrose, and today it's fully renovated and being operated in partnership with Roots Recovery as a women's and kids' shelter—quite a change from what that house used to be. What's extra awesome about this one is that Fila, the former trafficker who ran the brothel, helped us with the renovation and is now wholly on our side of this fight.

The trap house on Woodward Street has all the old bullet holes patched up and is fully renovated as well, providing a home to a survivor of many horrible things, her daughters, and a niece or two that she fosters from time to time.

Tweet survived the shooting that happened the day we shut Woodward down and has been waiting patiently on a job with us. He's put his old life of slinging dope behind him, as has Verdell, who now drives a truck for a living when he's not running the auto-detailing business we helped him start.

We've had some amazing people come to those streets, from Lt Col Stuart Scheller to one of the original Horse Soldiers, Billy Howell of ODA 515, to Jody Plauche, son of legendary vigilante Gary Plauche.

Local celebrity and News Anchor, Joe Birch, did an amazing piece on our work. He called it "the most significant piece [he'd] ever covered in his twenty-plus years in news," and that piece led to some pretty unexpected alliances.

The West Tennessee Violent Crime and Drug Task Force, made initially aware of us because of a Once American anti-pedo tee shirt, requested a sit down with us, and followed up by asking us to speak at their conference in 2024. From there, multiple law enforcement agencies and state elected officials became aware of our work and wanted to get involved. This was the same Drug Task Force who arrested me on that big felony warrant in 2014. Today, they believe in rehabilitation ahead of incarceration when it comes to addicts and have become one of our strongest advocates in the local community.

In fact, our latest "big thing" is a direct result of the partnership between We Fight Monsters and the Drug Task Force. I informed my followers in a post on February 19, 2025:

> For years, Jess and I have dreamed of changing South Memphis - and Memphis as a whole - into a place where love, rather than hate; unity rather than violence, neighbors working together rather than fighting; meeting needs rather than judgement or politics, and beauty rather than blight are the things it's known for.
>
> We came off the streets of South Memphis, at some points victims of many of the calamities that plague the area - violent crime, childhood sexual abuse, property crime, poverty, hunger and homelessness - and at other points we were part of the problem, addicts pumping obscene amounts of money into the dope economy that fuels the calamity.
>
> We have an intimate understanding of the issues facing that community - narcotics and human trafficking, racial tensions, lack of economic opportunity, tragically high infant mortality rates, and on and on.
>
> Once we got clean, we honed some old skills into gifts to be used in efforts through our work in Afghanistan, Ukraine, Haiti, Mexico, and more - we established world-class teams of humanitarians and began building an army of sorts, one that uses human connection rather than weapons, and one that seeks to recruit opponents rather than eliminate them.
>
> As our work in South Memphis began, we laser-focused our efforts

on Melrose Street, until we had stopped ALL narco and sex trafficking on that block, and had acquired a number of former "dope houses" and turned them into "hope houses" where members of our army could begin rebuilding their lives.

It didn't take long to notice the sprawling 76,000sqft vacant facility that shares a property line with many of these hope houses.

Through local community partners in the DA's office, we were introduced to the owner of this property, Ms. Vanecia Belser Kimbrow, Esq, a seasoned real estate attorney with LOADS of experience renovating large commercial properties - who turns out to have the exact same vision for it as we do.

We are PROUD to announce a partnership with her and the River Region Development Fund to turn this blighted facility into a TREATMENT CENTER!!!!

-Comprehensive Treatment Programs: intensive inpatient care, outpatient programs, partial hospitalization, medical detox, 28-day rehab, and long-term residential programs.

-Trade School: Integrating trade school training into the facility, enabling more individuals to gain the skills needed for self-sufficiency.

-Community Collaboration Hub: Creating a central hub for partnerships with law enforcement, rehabilitation services, and local businesses to combat drug and human trafficking – always promoting rehabilitation over incarceration."

Ben and Lt. Col Stu Scheller

WE FIGHT MONSTERS

Ben in Lahaina

Lahaina - damage from the fires

Wynne Arkansas tornado damage

Ben and Jacob Owen - Wynne Arkansas tornados

Arezo, in Memphis - Her 23rd birthday - the first one she has ever celebrated.

Ben Owen doing The Shawn Ryan Show Episode 178

Ben and Jessica Owen - Before and After

CONCLUSION
WE. FIGHT. MONSTERS.

We means community. It means not walking alone. Jess and I spent nearly three decades chasing hope in the bottom of a bottle or the haze of a high, but it wasn't until we turned outward—toward others—that we found what we were really looking for. Our lives began to change when we stopped asking, *"How do I get better?"* and started asking, *"Who can I help?"*

We found purpose not in perfection, but in service. We've taken the same energy we once used to chase a high and repurposed it—to meet needs, to rescue, to restore. We built "hope houses" where there used to be brothels and dope spots. We got dealers out of the game and into real life. We've helped hundreds of people off the streets, out of the system, and into a future they never thought possible. And it wasn't magic. It was community. It was *we*.

Fight means this doesn't end. You don't "win" recovery. You don't check a box and coast. The battle is daily—hourly, even. We still show up because we promised we would. Years ago, we prayed, "God, get us out of hell—together—and we'll spend the rest of our lives coming back for those we left behind." That promise wasn't poetic. It was desperate. It was sacred. And it's what keeps us coming back, even when it's hard, even when it hurts.

CONCLUSION

We've fought in Afghanistan, in cartel territory, in courtrooms, and on street corners. We've fought to save lives the Taliban didn't want saved, and fought systems that didn't want to change. But the most important fight is the one we fight every day—against relapse, against complacency, against hopelessness.

Monsters are real. They take the form of pills, powder, and needles. But they also wear other faces—trauma, shame, isolation, self-hatred. Drugs are a monster not because they're tempting, but because they *work*. They numb the pain. They make the chaos quiet. And when you take them away, you feel *everything*—and it's too much. That's why people go back. Not because they want to die, but because they don't know how to live without the filter.

To leave drugs behind, you have to face something even scarier than the addiction itself. For us, that monster had a name. For others, it looks different. But make no mistake—every addict has to stare one down. And if you're going to help someone recover, you need to understand what they're really up against.

Monsters are cunning. They're persistent. And they don't go quietly. You don't defeat them once—you fight them every single day. But when you do it together, when you fight with purpose, when you *see the monster clearly*, you start to win more than you lose.

CONCLUSION

ACKNOWLEDGEMENTS

In no way is this list exhaustive, between my ADHD, compressed time lines, lost brain cells, and the chaos that is our life, I honestly didn't even want to attempt an acknowledgements page because I KNOW I'm going to leave out some critically important people and the LAST thing I ever want to do is to hurt feelings. But, there have been so many important people that we would be dead without, that we HAVE to attempt this.

To God, all the glory goes to You. Everything we have and everything we are came from You and belongs to You. We are but stewards of Your gifts and Your grace, to serve and to love as You have commanded us to.

To Erin, if you'd handled one single thing differently, I'd be dead and we wouldn't have made it. To her mother, Diane, who so eloquently reframed addiction and relapse in the context of cancer, remission, and recurrence for me before she lost her own battle with cancer. You two taught me that addiction isn't something to be ashamed of, nor controlled by.

To our children: Jackson, Maddy, Jacob, Lily, Joshua, Joseph, and James we love you all more than words can adequately describe. You all endured things that no child should ever have to and for that, we are truly sorry. But we are hopeful that through your experiences, it has given you a broader understanding of love, forgiveness, perseverance, the grace of God, and the fact that no one is beyond redemption. To Ava - Our wonderful little surprise, God willing, you will never know addicted parents, and for that we are grateful.

To my parents, Steve and Melanie, you always acted in love and did the best you could with the information available to you, without the foundation you laid for me, the example you set, and the lifeline you extended us in our darkest hour, we wouldn't have made it.

To Tony and Stephanie Shelby, for a decade now I have strived to find the peace and serenity that you two have. Thank you for entrusting your legacy to us to carry on, and for loving us until we learned to love ourselves.

To Judge Dwyer, Angela Parkerson and the Shelby County Drug Court team, thank you for allowing me to suffer the consequences of my actions and allowing me the opportunity to redeem myself on the other side of my journey.

To Bryan Owens...man, I don't have the words. THANK YOU for being in my corner, no matter when, where or what. Just... THANK YOU.

To Robert and Becca Coleman, thanks for embarking on an insane journey and fight that wasn't even yours to help a guy you barely knew get sober.

To Scott and Monty Mann, thank you for taking Jess and I under your wing, mentoring us, and believing in us. We wouldn't be where we are today if not for y'all, nor would we know how to navigate ANY of this.

To Randy Surles and Laura Graves, thank you for helping us get this story out and into words.

To Ernest Nisperos, Travis Peterson, David Hicks, Josh Jenkins, Amy Sins, Dan Robitaille, Matt Young, Joel Velazquez, Kristin Vaughn, Kevin Metcalf, Kevin Branzetti, Joe Scaramucci, Heather Collins, Chaz Kennedy, Radhe and Amrta, Jim Cole, the myriad of three letter agents and operatives we can't name, the SOF (both active and veteran), THANK YOU for trusting a couple of crackheads to work alongside you in some wild exploits around the world and domestically, many of which can't be told outside of our Signal chats.

To Jazz Cannon and Legend, from Kabul to Vienna, from Franklin to San Diego, thank you for standing up for what's right and being a couple of very solid friends in bad places.

To David and Tammy Johnson, and Rob Downey, THANK YOU for being spiritual guides and helping us model Christ in all we do.

To Johnie Carter and Jackie Condrey, thanks for believing in us and opening so many new doors for our work.

To Cody and Kasey Ables, you two came along right on time and helped redefine and renew our mission, filling our souls while shouldering a load we could no longer bear alone.

To Bubba, Tiffany, Matt, Bobbitt, Snead, Marcus, Cresia, Jade, Shelby, Coop, Moody, Chad, Big Red, Garland, Nicole, Farley, Officers Greer and Canter, HSI Midsouth, and the rest of our Memphis Army – thank you for helping us fight this war!

ABOUT THE AUTHORS

Ben and Jess Owen are parents to eight (sometimes ten), grandparents to one, humanitarians, fighters of evil, bringers of hope, formerly addicted, alcoholic and homeless. They're also co-founders of two non-profits—We Fight Monsters and Flanders Fields—that help people in some of the worst places in America and the world. Ben loves sharing that Jess can drive, load, and fire a M18 Hellcat, a WWII tank destroyer. He's also the only crackhead ever invited to CIA headquarters. When they're not in South Memphis helping others rebuild their lives after addiction, Ben and Jess can be found in rural Georgia where they live with their family.

www.wefightmonsters.org